The

Quantum-Karmic
Multiverse

Nadim Hamdan

To all seekers:

As you browse through this book,
you will come across hints of the 'theory of everything'.

Are you ready to explore?

General Disclaimer

This book, "The Quantum-Karmic Multiverse," is intended to provide helpful and informative material on the subjects discussed. It is shared with the understanding that the author and publisher are not engaged in rendering professional services in the book. If the reader requires personal assistance or advice, a competent professional should be consulted.

The author and publisher specifically disclaim any responsibility for any liability, loss, or risk, personal or otherwise, that is incurred as a consequence, directly or indirectly, of the use and application of any of the contents of this book. While every effort has been made to ensure the accuracy of the information contained in this book as of the date of publication, the author and publisher assume no responsibility for errors, inaccuracies, omissions, or for any change in the content herein due to changes in laws, regulations, practices or universe shifts.

In case elements contained in this book are unacceptable for you or offend your feelings, please be assured that this is not our intention. This book is substantially about the adventure of discovery of the infinite realm of unconditional love. We pray you will discover this essential message for yourself.

♡

Foreword

Dear Explorer Embarking on a Sacred Journey of Growth,

With a heart full of gratitude, I welcome you on a shared journey—one that is less about the pages you turn and more about the internal strides you make toward growth and evolution. Your readiness to venture into the realms of new paradigms serves as a beacon that guides authors on their path of co-creation. For your open heart and mind, I am truly grateful.

"The Quantum-Karmic Multiverse" stands as a portal to the spiritual world, a starting point for novices to witness the profound and elaborate interplay of existence.

My own path is deeply interwoven with diverse cultures and bodies of knowledge, from the meticulous domain of German corporate life in Information Technology and Organization Management to the mystical echoes of Yogic teachings, and the primordial call of the Amazon Jungle. This has set me on a profound voyage across the vast spectrum of life's experiences, but it was my professional interest in the future of Information Technology and computing, particularly in the revolutionary realm of quantum computing, that drew me into the intricacies of quantum mechanics, the cornerstone science that underpins this book. Alongside a network of brilliant minds, scholars, and scientists, it has been the entheogenic sacred medicine and the ancient wisdom of the teacher trees that have emerged as my most enlightening mentors. Their profound teachings have been instrumental in shaping my understanding, guiding me through the unseen world that connects all forms of life and consciousness.

The inception of this book was an attempt to chart my own understanding of the vast, intricate cosmos. It began as a private endeavor, a means to unravel and make sense of the profound complexities that shape our universal experience. As the narrative unfolded, it became clear that the insights gained could be of service to others, especially those with whom I co-create within the regenerative movement. With this realization, the book's purpose grew beyond my personal quest, aspiring to provide guidance to fellow seekers as they embark on their own spiritual journeys.

This work is, at its core, an introduction. The complexities that underlie our spiritual universe are vast, and while this book aims to guide us through the beginnings of understanding, it is but the opening of a door to the overwhelming cosmos of the spirit. The narrative traverses numerous scientific domains. For beginners, it may be necessary to embark on further research to fully grasp the extensive concepts presented. The **Glossary** provided within these pages, along with the recommended further readings, will prove to be invaluable resources for delving into the intricacies of these diverse sciences.

Composing this book, particularly in English, which is not my native tongue, presented a considerable challenge, especially in sustaining a coherent narrative throughout the complex subject matter at hand. The AI large language models were instrumental in overcoming these hurdles. However, this AI assistance did not come without its difficulties. The AI, with its leanings toward certain biases, including a discernible politically non-neutral inclination, added layers of complexity to the task. Navigating these biases to maintain a neutral and unbiased stance demanded a heightened level of scrutiny and a deliberate, guiding hand. It was a meticulous process of shaping the AI's output to serve the book's purpose — to present a unifying narrative that transcends individual perspectives and resonates with a diverse readership.

In this context, as artificial intelligence integrates into the very sinews of our lives, this book acknowledges AI as a profound tool. It underlines that AI, much like a compass to a navigator, enhances our journey without dictating the destination. It's a reminder that, while AI deepens our interaction with the world, it remains a facilitator of human endeavor, not its replacement or purpose.

Now, you may ponder for whom is this narrative crafted? And why choose the present moment for its unveiling? The voice of this book extends its call to the seekers, the intellectually restless, the spiritual adventurers, and any individual attuned to the subtle yet profound shifts in our collective consciousness. As we stand at a historic inflection point, with the old giving way to the new, this discourse emerges as a timely compass. It's a dialogue that not only bridges but also harmonizes the mystical dance between quantum mechanics and ancient lore, connecting the analytical prowess of science with the intuitive depths of spirituality.

Drawing inspiration from pioneers like Ervin Laszlo and Amit Goswami, who have delved into the intersections of science and mysticism, this book aims to carve its niche by offering a deeply personal synthesis. With immense gratitude, I acknowledge the influence of such scholars, the wisdom keepers encountered during retreats on my four-year global journey, and most profoundly, the entheogenic teacher trees. While my narrative is rooted in established currents of thought, it seeks to differentiate by focusing on actionable, personal transformations that each one of us can embark upon, guided by the wisdom of these revered mentors and the transformative power of nature's own sages.

In the vibrant tapestry of this book, the metaphor of dance, prevalent in atomic physics and quantum mechanics, serves as a recurring theme to demystify the complex interplay of the universe's most fundamental forces. This dance metaphor is not merely a stylistic choice but a deliberate tool to illuminate the often intangible principles of quantum physics. By likening the behavior of particles and energies to a well-choreographed dance, we can envision the dynamic interactions that govern the cosmos in a more tangible, relatable way. This metaphor repeats throughout the book to reinforce the idea that the universe, at its core, is a harmonious and intricately connected dance of existence. It helps to bridge the gap between abstract scientific concepts and our everyday understanding, allowing the reader to grasp the profound truths of The Quantum-Karmic Multiverse in a manner that is both enlightening and familiar.

This book may serve as a catalyst for introspection and, at times, may challenge your perceptions. Should you find yourself triggered, remember this work is an offering, akin to a supermarket's variety — you are at liberty to choose what resonates and leave what does not. If such moments arise, I invite you to revisit this Foreword! The chapter on Decentralized Governance, in particular, may provide a comforting reframing of the principles that guide this journey.

Moreover, I encourage you to actively engage with the material presented, especially claims that may appear as hard facts. Utilize web search engines, and AI tools, or delve into the books recommended in the further readings section. There's no compulsion to take the author's word as sacrosanct; instead, rely on the most current scientific understandings and your own discerning common sense to forge your path through the information provided.

You are welcome to accept this loving invitation to embark on a journey filled with both caution and wonder, recognizing it as the mere beginning of an expansive exploration. Let your heart swell with anticipation and your spirit be enlivened by the promise of discovery that lies within these pages. This book is not just a path but a gateway, opening up to a grander expanse where every step forward is an act of love—a dance with the infinite. As you embrace this adventure with your eagerness to learn and grow, I pray your journey may be as rewarding as the destinations you dream of reaching.

With deepest respect and in the spirit of unity ♡

Nadim Hamdan

Contents

Introduction:

Dear fellow traveler,

Welcome to a grand exploration - a journey that traverses the realms of quantum mechanics, delves into the wisdom of Eastern philosophies, and uncovers the transformative power of personal growth. This journey will not be a solitary one. We are all participants in a cosmic dance, an intricate ballet of energy, consciousness, and existence that shapes our reality.

As we embark on this journey through 'The Quantum-Karmic Multiverse', it's important to acknowledge the intricate nature of the cosmos and our spiritual existence within it. To make these complexities more approachable, I invite you to think of this book as a map, one that guides you through a vast and mystifying landscape of spiritual and quantum realms. Just like a traveler in a new land, you may find some paths familiar and others utterly new and bewildering. My aim has been to chart these territories, providing you with a starting point to explore the labyrinth of the spirit. This book is like the opening of a door, revealing just the first few steps into an immense, uncharted territory. While it introduces fundamental concepts, the full understanding of our spiritual universe is an ongoing journey, inviting you to further exploration, research, and personal introspection.

In this book, I invite you to join me on this intense journey, delving into the heart of this cosmic dance. We will explore a theory christened as "Quantum-Karmic Multiverse Resonance," a proposition that every conscious being, through their karmic evolution, shapes and molds their unique personal universe. Each personal universe, with its unique vibrations and karmic imprints, contributes a singular note to the grand symphony of the multiverse.

I understand that each one embarking on this journey is at a different point in our spiritual exploration. Some of you may have already dipped your toes into the vast ocean of spiritual wisdom, while others may be standing on the shore, ready for the first immersive dive. I value and respect where you are in your journey and aim to provide insights that are illuminating for both novice and seasoned explorers alike.

This journey is not merely a theoretical exploration. It is a call to action, a guidebook filled with practical tools and insights drawn from a rich tapestry of wisdom - from Yogic, Indian, Tibetan, Taoist, Shamanic, and Sufi traditions to the pioneering theories of modern science. It is an invitation to understand and tap into the power of your intentions, thoughts, and emotions, to align your personal universe with the greater multiverse, and to dance in harmony with the cosmic rhythm.

As we set forth on this shared path of discovery, we will delve into the principle of Karma, explore the role of vibrations and frequencies, and understand the impact of our consciousness on the universe. We will navigate the dance of duality, align with the greater multiverse, and discover practical tools to facilitate this alignment. We will journey through astral realms, explore sacred geometries, and tap into the transformative power of entheogens. We will trace the soul's journey, understand the alchemy of emotions, and tap into the echoes of eternity.

This journey is an invitation to each one of us - to step onto the cosmic dance floor, to move to the rhythm of the multiverse, and to weave our unique dance into the cosmic choreography. So, dear reader, shall we dance?

Let us begin this journey, dear reader, not as separate individuals but as fellow dancers in the cosmic ballet, each learning, growing, and evolving, together in the grand dance of the Karmic Multiverse. Let us embrace the Cosmic Dance.

In the grand ballet of existence, a tale unfolds,
A cosmic dance, a journey through countless folds.
Quantum and Karma, a dance entwined,
In the cosmic rhythm, their steps aligned.

Navigating the personal universe, a dance of delight,
Attracting what we harbor, in the cosmic night.
Through the tides of emotion, a transformation takes form,
In the cosmic ballet, a new dance is born.

A theory of everything, a cosmic verse,
In the dance of the multiverse, we immerse.
In the cycle of reincarnation, a soul takes flight,
In the cosmic rhythm, it dances day and night.

Through transformation and growth, our dance takes form,
In the echoes of eternity, a new dance is born.
Mastering our destiny, the artist's brush,
In the cosmic canvas, a serene hush.

Chapter 1:
The Quantum-Karmic Connection

"Quantum theory will not look ridiculous to people who have read Vedanta."

- Werner Heisenberg

Quantum Mechanics and Karma

In the grand ballet of the cosmos, where galaxies pirouette and stars shimmer in rhythmic choreography, lies a profound truth that has echoed in the sacred halls of sages and sparked the curiosity of philosophers for millennia. It's a truth woven into the very fabric of existence, hinting at the intricate interplay of energies, frequencies, and consciousness that gives birth to the multiverse. This cosmic dance is not merely a spectacle for us to observe from afar, but an event in which every conscious being is an active participant, each weaving their own unique rhythm into the grand choreography of existence.

As we step onto the cosmic dance floor, let's first explore a fascinating intersection where modern science meets ancient wisdom. Here, in the realm of quantum mechanics and the principle of Karma, we find a profound connection - a dance of energy and intent that shapes our personal universe.

The Dance of Energy and Intent

Quantum Mechanics, the science that describes the behavior of particles at the smallest scales, paints a picture of reality that's very different from our everyday experiences. It suggests a world where particles can exist in multiple places at once, influence each other instantaneously over vast distances and even shift between states just by being observed.

These peculiar behaviors have challenged our understanding of reality and sparked a revolution in scientific thought.

Parallel to these quantum wonders, the principle of Karma, deeply rooted in Eastern philosophies, portrays a cosmic law of cause and effect. It proposes that every thought we harbor, every emotion we feel, and every action we undertake leave an indelible mark on the fabric of our personal universe. These imprints, born from this life and carried over from past lives, influence the trajectory of our karmic evolution.

Despite their different origins - one from modern science, the other from ancient wisdom - quantum mechanics and Karma share a profound resonance. Both suggest a universe that's intimately responsive to our actions, a reality that's woven by our conscious and unconscious choices. Like dancers moving to the same beat, they depict a universe that's not deterministic, but one full of potentialities, shaped by consciousness and intent.

The Observer Effect and Conscious Reality Creation

One of the most intriguing elements of quantum mechanics is the 'observer effect,' which posits that the act of observation influences what is being observed. This principle challenges the conventional view of consciousness as a passive spectator and suggests that it is an active participant in the creation and transformation of reality.

This idea of conscious reality creation resonates deeply with the Quantum-Karmic Multiverse Resonance. It suggests that our personal universes, shaped by our consciousness and karmic imprints, can influence and be influenced by the greater multiverse. As conscious beings, our intentions, thoughts, emotions, and actions shape our personal universe, adding a unique rhythm to the cosmic dance.

Non-Locality and the Cosmic Web

One of the most awe-inspiring and counterintuitive principles to emerge from quantum mechanics is the concept of non-locality. It challenges our classical intuition and thrusts us into the realm where space and time no longer constrain the interconnection of entities.

Non-locality refers to the phenomenon where particles that have once interacted, regardless of the distance separating them, seem to influence each other instantaneously. Einstein famously dubbed it "spooky action at a distance," finding it hard to reconcile with his relativity theory. However, experiments, notably Bell's theorem experiments, have repeatedly confirmed this quantum strangeness.

Many spiritual traditions and schools of thought propose that consciousness itself might be non-local, distributed across the etheric field, and transcendent of our physical confines. This aligns with the Akashic Records' concept, suggesting that our experiences, thoughts, and emotions aren't limited to the individual but are part of a grand cosmic database accessible to all at certain levels of consciousness. More about Ether and the Akashic Records later in the book.

The Holographic Universe and the Net of Indra

The Holographic Principle is presented from a scientific perspective as a groundbreaking concept that revolutionizes our understanding of reality. This theory suggests that our perceived three-dimensional universe might actually be a two-dimensional projection, akin to a hologram. Originating from the fields of quantum physics and cosmology, particularly in the study of black holes and information theory, the Holographic Universe posits that all the information constituting our 3D 'reality' could be encoded on a 2D surface. This aligns with the principles of quantum mechanics, especially the phenomena of quantum entanglement and non-locality, indicating an inherent interconnectedness and suggesting that each part of the universe contains a complete picture of the whole.

This concept echoes the ancient wisdom of Indra's Net, a metaphorical net from the Avatamsaka Sutra of Mahayana Buddhism. Visualize a vast cosmic net that stretches infinitely in every direction. In each junction of this net, there's a jewel, each reflecting all the other jewels in this cosmic lattice. This concept illustrates the interconnectedness of the universe and all beings within it. Each jewel in the net represents an individual life form, event, or object in the universe. The reflection in each jewel is the representation of all other forms, events, and objects in the universe. This metaphor signifies that everything is interconnected; every action, thought, and occurrence has a ripple effect throughout the entire net, affecting the whole in some way.

Just as each jewel in Indra's Net reflects the entirety of the cosmic web, each personal universe - shaped by the interplay of quantum phenomena and karmic resonance - is a full holographic fragment of the greater multiverse. Each of us carries not only our own karmic trajectory but also an echo of the whole, subtly entangled with every other expression of life. In this view, personal universes are not isolated realities, but radiant nodes in the infinite net - each one influencing, and being influenced by, all others.

Dancing with Paradox
and the Multidimensional Map

As we begin our exploration of the quantum-karmic connection, we stand at the precipice of a profound understanding. We've journeyed through the realms where science and spirituality converge, witnessing the cosmic ballet of energies, frequencies, and consciousness. Our role in this grand choreography is not that of mere spectators, but of active participants - each of us weaving a unique rhythm into the multiverse.

Yet, as we transition into the next chapter, it is essential to honor the multidimensional complexity of the universe. The concepts we are exploring are not linear lessons, but threads in a vast, cosmic tapestry - interwoven, reverberating, and often appearing again from new angles, with new frequencies. You may notice the return of themes you thought you had already met. This is not redundancy; it is resonance. Just as particles oscillate in harmonic patterns, the universe teaches by rhythm, echo, and recursive insight.

Most notably, you will see the metaphor of the dance arise again and again. This is deliberate. The dance is not only a symbol - it is a method. It embodies movement, creative tension, release, and flow: all of which are essential to understanding the interplay of quantum mechanics, karma, and consciousness. It is through this metaphor that we attempt to translate the unspeakable into something our being can begin to feel.

And so, the invitation as you journey through these pages is to always remember that what you hold in your hands is not merely a book, but a multidimensional compass - a woven, living map to help you navigate the swirling paradoxes and shimmering illusions of existence. It is not a linear guide, but a subtle orientation tool within the intentionally paradoxical and often bewildering illusion we call reality. Like any good map of hidden terrain, it folds back in on itself, revealing new layers with each encounter. What once felt clear may blur, and what once confused may begin to shine. Let your intuition walk beside your intellect, allowing the rhythm of discovery to unfold in its own time.

In the grand ballet of existence, a truth profound,
Where science meets wisdom, a common ground.
In the realm of quantum, particles dance,
In the law of Karma, actions enhance.

Particles in places multiple, unseen,
In Karma, deeds echo in the cosmic scene.
Quantum and Karma, a dance so divine,
In realms unseen, yet within the soul's shrine.

Observer and observed, a dance entwined,
Reality shaped by the conscious mind.
In the Net of Indra, a cosmic reflection,
A universe of wonder, in every direction.

Chapter 2:
Navigating the Personal Universe

"The Many-worlds interpretation is the only completely coherent approach to explaining both the contents of quantum mechanics and the appearance of the world."

- Hugh Everett

Infodynamics, Information Physicality, and Quantum Gravity

A fundamental principle of infodynamics is the physicality of information. Information resulting from our thoughts, intentions, and emotions carries physical properties, similar to mass and energy. This principle aligns with quantum mechanics and karma, signifying that our conscious decisions actively influence reality.

Take the example of planning a trip to a new city. The thoughts about places to visit, times to go, and activities to do all generate information. In the realm of infodynamics, these thoughts aren't just abstract ideas but possess physical properties and generate accordingly Karma. As the plans get refined, the behavior of this information system changes, actively shaping a portion of the universe.

In the context of Quantum-Karmic Multiverse Resonance, quantum gravity takes on a metaphysical dimension. We can envision karmic forces as a form of "quantum gravity" that shapes our personal universes and influences their interaction with the multiverse. Just as physical objects are bound by the pull of gravity, our generated information (karma) has a pull on our realities.

In the cosmic ballet, infodynamics introduces a new rhythm where every piece of information - be it a thought, intention or emotion - plays a role in shaping the universe. The interplay of quantum mechanics, karma, and infodynamics positions us not merely as observers, but as active contributors to the cosmic narrative within a grand simulation. More about simulation will be expounded in the next chapters.

Karma as Information: The Physical and the Infinite

You, as an individual, are more than just your physical body. Your true self is a part of something far greater - an infinite reality that extends beyond the physical realm. However, our karmic imprints keep us anchored to our bodily existence. This tethering is not inherently negative; it provides a sense of security and continuity. But it's important to remember that we are not limited to this physical form. The exploration of our true, infinite nature, unbound by the physical constraints imposed by karma, will be a central theme in the later chapters of this book. We will delve deeper into how we can recognize and transcend these limitations, connecting more profoundly with the boundless essence of our being.

Karma: The Double-Edged Sword

Karma acts as a double-edged sword. On one side, it provides a structured framework for our existence, ensuring that the universe operates under a system of cause and effect. This structure is essential for our growth and learning. However, on the other side, karma can act as a barrier, preventing us from experiencing the full extent of our true, infinite nature. In navigating this process, it is vital to remember that you are always safe. Your existence, bound as it is by karma, is part of a larger, protective mechanism that maintains the order of your personal universe. This understanding can provide immense comfort and reassurance as you explore the deep depths of your being and this book.

The Power of Suggestion, Law of Attraction, and Positive Affirmations

At the heart of our personal universe lies the potent interplay of suggestion and the Law of Attraction, both governed by the principles of Karma and quantum gravity. They operate on the understanding that our consciousness - thoughts, beliefs, and expectations - profoundly impacts our reality, attracting experiences aligned with our mental and emotional states.

Suggestion and the Law of Attraction function on both conscious and subconscious levels. Conscious suggestions, such as goal-oriented thoughts or positive affirmations, are intentionally imposed. Subconscious suggestions, more nuanced, are absorbed from our environment, upbringing, and social conditioning. Both shape our reality and participation in the cosmic dance.

The placebo effect, often seen in healthcare, is an impressive demonstration of these principles. When an individual believes in the effectiveness of a treatment, even if it's inactive or neutral, their health can improve purely based on their belief. This effect illustrates the power of suggestion and how our thoughts and beliefs can manifest into physical reality.

Positive affirmations are a powerful tool to harness these forces. These optimistic statements help us reshape thought patterns and manifest desired changes. Affirmations about self-love, prosperity, health, and peace align our thoughts and emotions with our intentions, interweaving positivity into the cosmic dance.

Our thoughts, beliefs, and affirmations ripple beyond our personal universe, influencing the collective consciousness. They underscore the interconnectedness of all things and our role as co-creators of reality.

The Alchemical Process of Emotional Transformation

Emotions, from the bliss of love to the despair of grief, each create information and karma, carrying a unique vibrational frequency. These frequencies can resonate with the energies of the multiverse, influencing our personal universe and our dance within the cosmic choreography. However, emotions are not merely vibrations to be experienced and expressed. They are also opportunities for growth and transformation - an alchemical process that can transmute base emotions into higher states of consciousness.

This emotional alchemy involves acknowledging our emotions without judgment, understanding their source, expressing them in healthy ways, and learning the lessons they bring. By embracing this alchemical process, we can transform our emotional energy into wisdom and personal growth, aligning ourselves more closely with the rhythms of the karmic multiverse.

Practical Emotional Mastery Techniques for Personal Growth

Emotional mastery involves developing skills and techniques to navigate our emotional landscape effectively. This includes mindfulness practices that help us stay present with our emotions, breathing exercises that can help regulate our emotional state, and journaling techniques that can provide insights into our emotional patterns.

One powerful technique is the "RAIN" method, which stands for Recognize, Allow, Investigate, and Non-Identification. This mindfulness-based approach encourages us to Recognize our emotions, Allow them to be present, Investigate their source and what they're trying to tell us, and maintain Non-Identification with the emotion, understanding that we are not our emotions.

By practicing emotional mastery, we can navigate the ebb and flow of our emotional tides with wisdom and grace, transforming our emotional energy into a powerful force for personal and karmic evolution. It's important for the serious seeker to approach this process with an intention not to create new karma. This means observing emotions as they arise without judgment and allowing them to pass like clouds, a deeper aspect of this practice that will be explored further in later chapters of the book.

The Personal Universe: A Cosmic Mirror

Imagine standing in front of a mirror. The reflection you see is a representation of you, but it's not the complete picture. It doesn't capture your dreams, your thoughts, your emotions, or your past experiences. Similarly, the personal universe is a holographic reflection of us within the multiverse. It includes not just our physical existence but also our thoughts, emotions, actions, and karmic imprints. It is a living, breathing, evolving manifestation of our consciousness.

In this chapter, we have journeyed through the personal universe, guided by the principles of infodynamics, karma, quantum gravity, and the Law of Attraction. We've seen how our thoughts, emotions, and intentions are not mere ephemeral entities but hold the power to shape the fabric of our reality. The understanding of our personal universe as a reflection and creation of our inner world brings with it a great responsibility and a profound opportunity. Reflect on a scenario in your life where the Law of Attraction seemed evidently at play. How did your thoughts, beliefs, and emotions align with the outcome you experienced?

As we segue into the next chapter, remember that the universe is a complex, multidimensional entity, echoing its truths across various planes. The overlap of concepts between chapters is intentional, mirroring the universe's method of reinforcing its intricate patterns. We reencounter these ideas in different forms to deepen our understanding and to appreciate the multifaceted nature of our existence.

In the cosmic dance, we are the creators,
The architects of our universe, the navigators.
With every thought, every emotion, we sow,
A seed in our universe that will grow.

The law of attraction, a cosmic decree,
Like attracts like, in this grand sea.
Positive affirmations, the lighthouse in our night,
Guiding our personal universe to the light.

Mindful navigation, the compass in our hand,
Helping us understand where we stand.
Relationships and challenges, our teachers so wise,
Guiding our growth, as we rise.

Chapter 3:
Belief Systems - The Choreography of Our Cosmic Dance

"Your beliefs become your thoughts, your thoughts become your words, your words become your actions, your actions become your habits, your habits become your values, your values become your destiny."

- Mahatma Gandhi

The Invisible Choreographers

Belief systems are the fundamental principles that drive our actions, shape our perceptions, and influence our relationships with others and the universe at large. They are the unseen choreographers of our cosmic dance, silently orchestrating our moves, guiding our steps, and shaping our encounters in the karmic multiverse.

Formation of Belief Systems

Belief systems are the core values, assumptions, and attitudes we hold about ourselves, others, and the world around us. They are like the underlying software that runs the hardware of our minds, directing our thoughts, feelings, and behaviors. When we comprehend the nature and impact of our belief systems, we are better equipped to navigate our personal universe and engage in a more harmonious cosmic dance.

Our belief systems are not formed in a vacuum. They are shaped by a confluence of influences including our upbringing, cultural context, personal experiences, and innate tendencies. For instance, if we grow up in an environment that espouses the virtues of compassion and empathy, these values can form the cornerstone of our belief system.

The Power and Limitations of Belief Systems

Belief systems can serve as powerful guides in our cosmic dance, providing us with a sense of direction and purpose. They can inspire us to strive for higher ideals, motivate us to overcome challenges, and ground us in times of uncertainty.

However, belief systems can also limit our growth and restrict our dance. For example, if we hold a belief that we are unworthy or incapable, it can block our personal development and inhibit our potential. Similarly, a belief in a hostile universe can generate fear and a sense of isolation, disrupting our harmonious dance with the multiverse.

The Universality of 'Religiousness'

We are all 'religious' in a sense, not necessarily in the conventional understanding of adhering to a specific faith or belief system, but in the broader sense of having a structure of beliefs, values, and practices that give meaning to our lives. This 'religiousness' can manifest in myriad ways - it could be a mosque, a shopping mall, or a peaceful park that serves as your shrine; a family photo, an iPhone, or a cross that represents your sacred symbol; and New Year's Day, Sabbath or your own birthday that marks your special day.

The key understanding here is that 'religiousness' is a reflection of our consciousness - it is a manifestation of our intent, beliefs, and values. It is a part of our dance within the Karmic Multiverse, shaping our personal universe and rippling out into the greater cosmos.

Conscious Choice: The Architect of Your Universe

While we all participate in this cosmic dance, it's vital to understand that if we do not consciously choose our 'religion' - our beliefs, values, and practices - external influences such as societal norms, family traditions, peer pressures, media, education, or religious institutions may end up choosing for us. This is not a judgment, but a recognition of the power and importance of conscious choice.

As architects and designers of our personal universe, we have the freedom to choose how we dance in the multiverse. We can select the beliefs and practices that resonate with us, discard those that no longer serve us, and create our unique dance. This freedom of conscious choice is at the heart of our journey through the Karmic Multiverse.

Embodying your conscious choices involves aligning your intentions, thoughts, emotions, and actions with your chosen beliefs and practices. It means dancing your dance with authenticity, expressing your truth, and contributing your unique rhythm to the cosmic symphony.

Transforming Belief Systems and Vertical Time

Transforming limiting belief systems involves a conscious and deliberate process. It begins with identifying and acknowledging the beliefs that no longer serve our growth. This can be achieved through introspection, mindfulness practices, and therapeutic interventions.

Once these limiting beliefs are brought into awareness, we begin the sacred work of reshaping the energetic structure of our personal universe. Visualization, affirmation, cognitive reframing, emotional alchemy, and ritual become tools not merely of healing, but of energetic reprogramming. From a quantum-karmic perspective, this transformation is not confined to the surface mind - it reaches deep into the metaphysical fields of resonance, where belief is not a thought, but a frequency.

To truly understand the power of this work, we must now invoke the dimension of Vertical Time. In Vertical Time, transformation is not a journey from falsehood to truth - it is the conscious selection of which truth becomes your origin, and thus, your reality. The moment you anchor into a belief not as a wish, but as a knowing, your universe begins to reflect that knowing back to you. Not symbolically, but physically. The landscapes of your life, the events that unfold, the synchronicities that arrive, will all begin to echo your new creation story. And it doesn't stop there.

Other personal universes, other people, will be drawn to your vibration, and their stories will confirm your myth. Their pasts will somehow mirror yours. Their gods may wear the same face. Conversations will ripple with uncanny resonance, as if you are all remembering the same dream together. And those who no longer match your frequency may quietly drift away - no conflict, just a gentle divergence in the dance.

Even science - yes, even science - will begin to reveal discoveries that align with the very beliefs you once feared were too mystical, too strange, too sacred. Papers will be published. Theories will emerge. Archeological evidence may "suddenly" be found. But it is not science leading belief - it is your belief altering the configuration of the multiverse, selecting from infinite potentialities the version of reality that makes your inner knowing undeniably external.

This is not illusion. This is resonant co-creation. You are not bending truth - you are tuning into a truth that has always existed in potential, awaiting the strength of your belief to bring it into manifestation. Later in the book, we will explore "truth" and illusion more deeply, revealing the role of gods and prophets, not only as messengers from the Divine, but as powerful belief conductors, sculptors of karmic resonance, who seeded entire civilizations with origin stories powerful enough to call forth entire timelines, entire worlds. Perhaps you are such a being! What are the core beliefs that shape your perception of the universe, and where did they originate? Can you identify a belief you once held that you have since transformed, and how did that change affect your life's path?

In the vast theater of life's grand dance,
Silent choreographers lead our advance.
Belief systems, unseen, guide our stance,
In the cosmic waltz of chance and circumstance.

These guides, subtle, shape our view,
Influencing all that we think and do.
Yet they can trap us, limiting and askew,
Till we choose anew, in life's endless renew.

By conscious choice, we architect our way,
Crafting beliefs that brighten our day.
In the quantum dance, our spirits sway,
Transforming our path in a luminous ballet.

Chapter 4:
Boundaries, Bridges, and Resonant Reflection

"The unity and continuity of Vedanta are reflected in the unity and continuity of wave mechanics. This is entirely consistent with the Vedanta concept of All in One."

- Erwin Schrödinger

The Role of Relationships and Challenges in Karmic Evolution

On our journey through the karmic multiverse, we encounter various companions and face many challenges. These are not random occurrences, but critical aspects of our karmic evolution.

Relationships, whether they manifest as friendships, family ties, or romantic partnerships, offer mirrors into our deepest selves. They reflect our strengths, illuminate our shadows, and provide opportunities for growth and transformation.

Similarly, challenges, whether they appear as obstacles, conflicts, or hardships, are catalysts for our growth. They push us out of our comfort zones, test our resilience, and guide us toward our highest potential. By embracing these relationships and challenges, we can navigate our personal universe with wisdom and compassion, and contribute to the cosmic dance in meaningful and transformative ways.

Boundaries of the Personal Universe: The Edge of Perception

The boundaries of a personal universe can be thought of as the limits of one's perception and influence. Just as a dancer has a personal space on the dance floor, each of us has a personal universe within the Karmic

Multiverse. These boundaries are not rigid walls but dynamic, fluid constructs, expanding and contracting based on our consciousness, experiences, and evolution.

While each personal universe has its boundaries, they are not impenetrable fortresses. They are porous and permeable, allowing influences to flow in and out. These exchanges occur through our interactions with others, our shared experiences, and our collective consciousness. Just as dancers influence each other through their movements and rhythm, personal universes interact and influence each other within the Karmic Multiverse.

At times, this interaction can become so potent, so magnetically charged, that two personal universes seem to momentarily merge or orbit in close resonance. This occurs in profound experiences such as the honeymoon phase of a romantic relationship, where the gravitational pull of attraction feels like the collapsing of boundaries and the birth of a shared field. In these moments, it's not merely two individuals falling in love - it's two universes folding into one dance, co-creating a temporary reality so vivid, so heightened, it alters the trajectory of both. The stronger the love, the attraction, the more pronounced the magical response of the universe - manifesting as synchronicities, living symbols, and even the reverent reactions of animals or strangers, as if the world itself pauses to honor the resonance unfolding between them.

Even more archetypally, the moment of birth is not only the emergence of a new human life but the creation of a wholly new personal universe. The mother, in that sacred passage, becomes the portal through which consciousness incarnates - birthing not just a body, but a cosmos. For a time, the child's universe exists within the mother's field, entirely interwoven with her presence, her breath, her being. It is only through gradual individuation that this new universe begins to take shape and self-direct.

These gravitational encounters - be they romantic, maternal, or spiritual - reveal that while personal universes are sovereign, they are also capable of extraordinary resonance. They remind us that within the Karmic Multiverse, we are never truly isolated; we are co-weavers of an ever-evolving web of shared reality.

Resonant Reflections: Co-Creating the Dance of Interpersonal Universes

The bridges between personal universes are built through connection. These connections can take various forms - relationships, shared experiences, empathy, and love. They serve as conduits for energy, information, and influence, linking personal universes and facilitating their dance within the Karmic Multiverse.

Our emotions do not exist in isolation. They resonate within our personal universe and ripple out into the multiverse, influencing and being influenced by the cosmic dance. For instance, feelings of love and compassion can resonate with higher frequencies, aligning us with experiences and realities that reflect these states.

In the intricate dance of the cosmos, our interactions with others play a pivotal role in the choreography of our personal universe. Every individual we encounter carries not just one, but an infinite spectrum of potential selves, each resonating with different aspects of the multiverse. The version of someone we interact with is, in part, a reflection of our own expectations, emotions, and energies - a mirror of our internal state projected onto the canvas of our shared reality.

When we meet another soul, it's as if two universes are brushing against each other, each with the power to influence the shape and texture of the other. The version of the person who steps into our world is co-created through this interaction. Our thoughts, feelings, and beliefs act as gravitational pulls, drawing out aspects of that person that resonate with our own frequency.

This phenomenon reveals a profound layer of responsibility in our relationships. By consciously cultivating emotions and intentions that resonate with the highest version of the individuals we meet, we invite the possibility of the higher self or supermind, to emerge more fully within our personal universe. We will explore more about this later in the book. If we approach others with suspicion and negativity, we may indeed draw forth a version of them that aligns with such energies. Conversely, when we meet them with openness, compassion, and a belief in their best selves, we encourage those very qualities to flourish in the space between us.

Thus, understanding the power of emotional resonance and intentional energy offers us a remarkable tool. It becomes a means to not only navigate but also co-create the emotional landscape of our interactions, encouraging the most positive and harmonious versions of those we encounter to present themselves. In doing so, we contribute to a shared dance that elevates the collective choreography of the multiverse.

Simulation Theory and the Virtual World

The principles of Simulation Theory, a contemporary philosophical and scientific construct, assert that our perceived reality is, in fact, a simulated or virtual construct. This intriguingly echoes the ancient spiritual depiction of the physical world as Maya, or illusion. This doesn't mean that it's not real, but rather it is not as we perceive it to be!

In this context, the concept of Back-Fill or Back-Drop people is further substantiated. These individuals, while integral to the narratives of our personal universes, do not possess an independent consciousness. Instead, they are essential elements of this grand simulation and extensions of ourselves. They contribute significantly to its complexity and depth. Their presence populates the world around us, enhancing the immersive nature of our simulated reality.

However, it is essential to acknowledge that incorporating this philosophy carries the risk of dehumanizing others. It should only be embraced when balanced with the yogic perspective - seeing all beings as one, recognizing them as our own self, and honoring this unity as sacred.

Recall a time when an encounter didn't go as you hoped. Considering the concept of resonant reflections, what might you change about your own approach or mindset to invite a more favorable version of the other person into your experience? Think of a recent interaction with someone where the outcome was positive and harmonious. How might your own emotional state and expectations have influenced the version of that person who showed up in your universe?

Emotions, the tides within our cosmic sea,
Each wave a frequency, a key.
In the dance of the multiverse, they sway,
Guiding our steps along the way.

An alchemical process, a transformative art,
Transmuting emotions, a journey of the heart.
From the depths of despair to the heights of joy,
Each emotion a thread in the cosmic ploy.

Techniques of mastery, the oars in our ride,
Helping us navigate the emotional tide.
With every breath, every beat, every notion,
We shape the multiverse with our emotion.

Chapter 5:
Free Will and Destiny

"Science cannot solve the ultimate mystery of nature. And that is because, in the last analysis, we ourselves are a part of the mystery that we are trying to solve."

- Max Planck

The Illusion and the Reality of Free Will

Welcome to a realm that weaves together the threads of destiny and choice, a dance floor on which the cosmic choreography of free will unfolds. The concept of free will invites us into a paradoxical dance, one that intertwines predetermination with the power of personal choice.

As we navigate the intricate maze of life, we often find ourselves at the crossroads of fate and free will. We wonder, "Am I the master of my destiny, or am I merely a puppet in the hands of an unseen cosmic puppeteer?" The question is profound, and the answer is nestled within the heart of paradox.

At first glance, free will might appear as an illusion, a mirage in the desert of determinism. After all, are we not shaped by our genetics, our upbringing, our environment, and the societal norms that dictate our lives? Moreover, modern neuroscience adds an even more unsettling layer to this mystery. Recent experiments reveal that our brain begins preparing to act several hundred milliseconds before we consciously make our decision. In other words, by the time we believe we are choosing, the choice may have already been made. This suggests that thought is more a commentator than a commander - a narrative that follows rather than leads the unfolding moment.

Other studies using fMRI technology have confirmed this uncanny insight: patterns of brain activity can predict a person's decision several seconds before they report consciously making it. You are always running behind reality, catching up to choices that have already been set in motion. This raises the unsettling possibility that what we perceive as "free will" is a delay - a story written in hindsight, not forged in real time.

The Quantum-Karmic Dance of Free Will

The quantum-karmic model of the universe offers a compelling lens through which to contemplate free will. Quantum mechanics presents us with the Uncertainty Principle, revealing that the very nature of reality is built on probability rather than certainty - suggesting, at first glance, an openness for conscious choice.

However, in the deeper architecture of the karmic multiverse, it is not our conscious mind that functions as the observer collapsing reality - it is karma itself. Our accumulated karma - formed from past actions, intentions, and unprocessed energies - acts as the true observer. It determines how the field of potentiality crystallizes into the present moment. The reality we perceive is not a blank canvas for the conscious will, but rather a karmically pre-rendered projection we step into, already colored by the imprints of what has come before.

Our consciousness often arrives after the fact. We believe we are steering, but more often, we are passengers. The events we encounter, the thoughts that arise, the emotions that surge - these are not freely summoned. They are karmic echoes we are living through. Reality, then, becomes a kind of sacred trap: it feels immediate, but it is already woven. What we call "now" is the harvest of past karmas, and we are always running slightly behind.

And yet, within this paradox lies the gateway to freedom. While we are not the conscious creators of the present moment, we are the creators of future karma. The only true agency we possess is the quality of our presence now - the awareness we bring, the intention we sow, the emotions we transmit into the field. In this way, we are always shaping the road ahead, even if we cannot rewrite the scene unfolding before us.

Free will, then, is not the power to dictate the moment, but the capacity to respond with awareness, and thus plant different seeds. It is the slow, sacred act of dissolving the trap by seeing it clearly, and choosing - with reverence - the next imprint we leave upon the fabric of the multiverse.

Mastering the Dance of Free Will

So, how do we master this cosmic dance of free will? Our first step is awareness. We must become conscious of our patterns, our reactions, and the impact they have on our personal universe and the greater multiverse.

Next, we cultivate mindfulness - a kind of radical presence in the moment - open and responsive to the rhythm of life. We learn to witness the karmic tides as they arise, and to respond from a place of clarity rather than compulsion. We learn to align our choices with the deeper music of the cosmos, making decisions that resonate with love, compassion, and gratitude.

Finally, we embrace responsibility - not as a burden, but as an empowering recognition of our creative potential. With each aware breath, each mindful gesture, each silent prayer of intention, we are sowing new karmas. And with these seeds, we shape our destiny.

As we journey through the karmic multiverse, let us remember: free will is not a force that controls the world, but a flame of consciousness that can illuminate the path ahead. It is our cosmic birthright, the rhythm of our becoming, and the silent author of the reality we have yet to live.

In a realm where destiny and choice entwine,
A cosmic dance where the divine divine,
Free will and fate in a paradox align,
In the grand ballet of the multiverse, they shine.

A puppet or master, in this life's design?
In the heart of the paradox, answers we find,
Neither illusion nor mere construct of the mind,
Free will, a reality, complex yet kind.

In the celestial ballet, free will and destiny bind,
Each step, each choice, in this dance assigned,
Free will, our cosmic birthright, divinely enshrined,
In the rhythm of existence, our spiritual sign.

Chapter 6:
Quantum Oscillations - A Key to Understanding

"Quantum physics thus reveals a basic oneness of the universe."

- Erwin Schrodinger

Quantum Oscillations:
The Synchronized Dance of Particles

This chapter stands at the heart of the book, offering crucial insights into the interconnected dance of particles in the universe. Understanding quantum oscillations is key to grasping the concepts of the Karmic Multiverse and how every aspect of our lives contributes to this grand cosmic dance. This chapter's ideas form the basis for many of the concepts explored in later chapters, making it a pivotal part of your journey through the book.

As we continue our dance within the Karmic Multiverse, we encounter a fascinating phenomenon at the heart of quantum mechanics - quantum coupled oscillator synchronization. This chapter explores how this quantum dance finds expression in art, music, beauty, and spiritual rituals, and how these expressions, in turn, influence the quantum field.

Quantum coupled oscillator synchronization refers to the phenomenon where two or more quantum systems begin to oscillate - or vibrate - in a synchronized manner. Much like dancers moving in perfect harmony, these quantum systems align their frequencies and rhythms, creating a synchronized dance at the quantum level.

To demystify this, imagine a grand orchestra where each musician (particle) plays in harmony with others, creating a symphony of existence.

Quantum Oscillations can be likened to this synchrony in music, where particles vibrate in a way that's perfectly aligned, much like notes in a melody. This phenomenon isn't just a scientific curiosity; it reflects the profound interconnectedness of all things, mirroring patterns found in nature, art, and spiritual practices. By understanding how these tiny particles dance together in unison, we gain insight into the fundamental principles that govern the cosmos and our place within it. This chapter aims to bring these high-level quantum concepts down to earth, relating them to everyday experiences and the world we see around us, making them more accessible and relatable.

The Dance of the Pendulums: Physical Manifestations of Synchronization

The concept of synchronization is not confined to the realm of quantum mechanics; it finds expression in physical phenomena as well. The synchronized oscillation of pendulums is one such manifestation.

Also known as coupled pendulum synchronization, is a striking example of how individual systems can spontaneously align their rhythms and frequencies. When two or more pendulums are attached to a common support, they can interact and begin to swing in unison. This phenomenon was first observed in the 17th century and has fascinated physicists and mathematicians ever since.

The synchronization of pendulums serves as a macroscopic model for understanding quantum-coupled oscillator synchronization. Just as pendulums can synchronize their swings, quantum systems can align their oscillations. However, unlike pendulum synchronization, which is mediated by a physical connection, quantum systems can synchronize even when spatially separated, a phenomenon known as quantum entanglement.

Art, Music, Beauty, and Rituals: The Quantum Symphony

Art, music, beauty, and spiritual rituals, in their various forms, reflect a form of quantum synchronization. They are expressions of rhythmic patterns, harmonious frequencies, and synchronized oscillations that resonate with our consciousness and evoke deep emotions. From the Tantric rituals of India that invoke divine energies to the Sufi practice of Dhikr, the repetitive chanting of divine names, these expressions and rituals help us align with the cosmic energies and shape our personal universe. In essence, they are dances of quantum oscillators, manifesting in our shared reality.

Influencing the Quantum Field through Frequency

Our engagement with art, music, beauty, and spiritual rituals doesn't merely evoke emotions - it also influences the quantum field. Our emotional responses, thoughts, and the resulting vibrational frequencies ripple out into the quantum field, contributing to the grand cosmic symphony. This interplay underpins the notion of Quantum-Karmic Multiverse Resonance, showing how our personal universe influences the greater multiverse.

We have delved into the synchronized dance of particles, a testament to the universe's intricate harmony. This understanding of quantum oscillations, the rhythmic pulse of the cosmos, brings us to an essential realization: it is our attention that powers these oscillations, directing the flow of energy and shaping our reality.

Now, we transition to the next chapter to explore the profound idea that our focus and consciousness are not just passive observers but active forces in the cosmic dance. Our attention, akin to a beam of light in the quantum realm, energizes the oscillations that weave the fabric of our existence. How do you perceive the idea that everything in the universe is interconnected?

In the cosmic ballet, a sight unseen,
Quantum oscillators, in a dance serene.
Moving in harmony, a rhythm so grand,
In the Karmic Multiverse, they make their stand.

Art, music, and beauty, a symphony divine,
Reflect the quantum dance, in rhythm and line.
Vibrations in harmony, frequencies align,
In the cosmic choreography, they shine.

Each note of music, each stroke of art,
Echos in the quantum field, playing its part.
In the Karmic Multiverse, our dance takes flight,
In the quantum field, we ignite the light.

Chapter 7:
The Power of Attention - Where Attention Goes, Energy Flows

"The more clearly we can focus our attention on the wonders and realities of the universe about us, the less taste we shall have for destruction."

- Rachel Carson

The Confluence of Attention and Energy

The universe is a dance of energy, a ceaseless flow of exchange and transformation that shapes the fabric of our reality. At the heart of this energetic ballet, guiding the ebb and flow is the power of our attention. "Where attention goes, energy flows," is a simple yet profound adage that underscores the pivotal role our focus plays in shaping our personal universe and contributing to the grand cosmic dance.

Attention, in its simplest form, is the act of consciously directing our mental focus toward a particular object, idea, or activity. It is through this act of attention that we interact with the world around us, perceiving and interpreting our surroundings. But attention goes beyond mere perception. It is a conduit for energy, serving as the channel through which our intentions, thoughts, and emotions flow into the world.

Where we direct our attention, we simultaneously direct our energy. Like a spotlight illuminating the stage, our attention highlights the areas of our lives where energy is invested. Whether it's a thought, a feeling, a goal, or a relationship, the focus of our attention becomes the recipient of this energy, influencing its development and transformation.

Mobilizing the Power of Attention

Recognizing the dynamic interaction between attention and energy is the first step toward harnessing the power of this relationship. By consciously directing our attention, we can guide the flow of our energy, shaping our experiences and influencing our reality.

When we focus on positive experiences, thoughts, and emotions, we channel our energy into these areas, amplifying their presence in our lives. Similarly, when we direct our attention toward negative or unproductive elements, we feed these aspects with our energy, allowing them to grow and dominate our experiences.

Understanding this, the power to shape our personal universe lies in our hands. By consciously choosing where to direct our attention, we decide where our energy flows, influencing the course of our life's dance.

The Ripple Effects in the Karmic Multiverse

In the karmic multiverse, the interplay of attention and energy takes on a cosmic scale. Our individual dances, guided by our attention, contribute to the grand ballet of the multiverse. Each thought, each emotion, each action - guided by our attention - sends ripples of energy into the etheric field, influencing the collective dance within the transpersonal space. More about this in the chapters ahead.

The knowledge of "where attention goes, energy flows" serves as a compass, guiding our journey. Through conscious attention, we can direct our energy toward harmony, unity, and growth, enriching our personal dance and contributing to the symphony of the multiverse. Think about an aspect of your life or a personal goal that you would like to develop or improve. How can you intentionally direct your attention to positively influence this area? Consider the areas of your life where you invest the most attention. How does this investment of attention serve you and your followers?

In the grand theatre of existence, under the cosmic glow,
Lies a truth profound and simple, essential to know.
"Where attention goes, energy flows," the sages often say,
A guiding light, a beacon bright, in life's intricate ballet.

Attention is a spotlight, in the theatre of the mind,
Illuminating corners, where energy is assigned.
Focus on the positive, and watch it grow and shine,
Neglect the seeds of sorrow, and joy may be thine.

Harnessing this power, with intent and mindful grace,
We become the sculptors, of our reality's face.
Directing the flow of energy, with attention's steady hand,
We shape and mold our experiences, in this mystic land.

Chapter 8:
Decentralized Governance - The Symphony of Quantum Synchronization

"The universe is a continuous web. Touch it at any point and the whole web quivers."

- Stanley Kunitz

Nature and Decentralized Governance

In the grand orchestra of the cosmos, a unique form of governance emerges that mirrors the principles of quantum mechanics. This isn't centralized, ruled by a singular entity, but a decentralized governance born of synchronized quantum oscillations. Each cosmic entity operates under a hierarchy of universal laws governing every particle and quantum oscillator. Yet within this, each cosmic entity contributes to the larger dance of existence, influencing and being influenced by the rest of the cosmos.

Consider a lush, sprawling rainforest: a complex, dynamic, and decentralized ecosystem where no single entity governs. Instead, a delicate balance between order and chaos is maintained, which allows for diversity and sustenance. In this decentralized governance system, each plant, animal, and microorganism plays its unique role. The tall trees provide canopies, the underbrush offers a fertile ground for other plants, insects play their part in pollination, and the predators keep the herbivore population in check.

Now, imagine a situation where a species of beetle, due to external factors, begins to multiply rapidly. This sudden increase (chaos) disrupts the balance, affecting the health of trees as they feed on their leaves and bark. The effects ripple throughout the ecosystem: birds who feed on these beetles find an abundant food source and increase in number, while trees become scarce, impacting herbivores dependent on them.

In time, natural decentralized governance mechanisms kick in. The rise in birds means more beetles get consumed, bringing their population down. As the beetle population declines, the trees begin to recover, restoring a semblance of order to the system. In this scenario, there isn't a single governing body that decides to intervene; instead, the ecosystem self-regulates through a dance of order and chaos.

Similarly, in the vast cosmos and our personal universes, a balance between order and chaos is essential. When embraced, chaos can lead to growth, evolution, and innovation, while order ensures structure, stability, and harmony. In a decentralized governance system, both elements are crucial. Like the rainforest, our personal universes, when influenced by external or internal factors, may swing between order and chaos. But through interconnectedness and the intrinsic principles of quantum synchronization, they find their way back to harmony within the grand cosmic symphony.

Cosmic Framework:
The Hierarchy of Universal Order

At the foundation of the universe lies the Source, a singular point from which all existence springs forth. This Source then expresses itself as duality, the yin and yang of the cosmos, which is the basic structure of all natural phenomena. Within this duality, there is a dynamic balance of order and chaos, each giving rise to the other, ensuring the constant evolution and vitality of the universe. From this interplay emerges a set of principles known as the Hermetic laws, a series of universal constants that govern the behavior of all things. These laws provide a predictable pattern within the apparent randomness of existence, much like the consistent rules of physics that underpin the chaotic behavior of quantum particles.

Guidance for the Lost:
Finding Direction in Cosmic Laws

For those feeling lost in the quantum wilderness, where reality is a fluctuation of possibilities, the Hermetic laws, and the elemental forces offer a grounding touchstone. When the principles of quantum mechanics challenge one's perception of reality, these ancient laws serve as a reliable compass. The seeker is advised to observe the Principle of Rhythm, which teaches that life is a series of ebbs and flows, much like the alternating cycles of yin and yang, order and chaos. By recognizing this rhythm, one can find solace in the predictability of these cycles, even in the midst of uncertainty. The elements - earth for stability, air for clarity, fire for transformation, water for adaptability, and ether for spiritual connection - provide a sensory way to align with these cosmic rhythms, acting as anchors to the universal principles that can guide one back to a sense of wholeness and direction.

Decentralized Governance and the Dance
of Personal Universes

Within the cosmic framework, our personal universes - encompassing our thoughts, emotions, and experiences - function as quantum oscillators. These oscillators do not simply operate in isolation but are energetically intertwined, just like Indra's Net, each resonating with a unique vibrational signature that interacts within the vast network of decentralized governance at the quantum level. The penetration through the cosmic hierarchy occurs not solely through the elevation of frequency but through the potency of our energetic emissions, whether they are high, low, or somewhere in between.

The universes charged with intense emotions - those of profound love, deep compassion, and sincere gratitude - carry a robust energy that reverberates powerfully within the quantum field. They have the capacity to mold the collective consciousness not through coercion but through the sheer force of their presence, encouraging a ripple effect that prompts other personal universes to attune to these dynamic energies.

Conversely, oscillators saturated with the lower frequencies of fear, shame, or anger also wield significant influence. These energies, though often viewed negatively, possess their own form of potency. They, too, can propagate through the collective, influencing the quantum tapestry with their intensity. It is in this interplay of varied frequencies and strengths that our personal universes shape and are shaped, contributing to the grand mosaic of existence.

Acknowledging the spectrum of these vibrational energies is vital. While higher frequencies are traditionally associated with constructive change, the lower frequencies serve as a contrast, highlighting areas of potential growth and healing. They remind us that the path through the hierarchy is not a one-way ascent but a complex journey requiring the navigation of the full range of emotional experiences. It is through this journey that wisdom is gleaned, resilience is built, and eventually, even the most turbulent frequencies can be harmonized and integrated into the symphony of the whole.

The Frequency of Art, Music, and Rituals

Art, music, and spiritual rituals, whether perceived as beautiful or ugly, harmonious or disharmonious, indeed serve as potent expressions of our quantum oscillations. They interlace with our consciousness, stir profound emotions, and shape the vibrational energy of our personal universes. This resonance is akin to the ancient concept of Indra's net, where each universe is a jewel, reflecting and interpenetrating every other. As such, the frequencies emanating from our engagement with art, music, and rituals extend into the quantum field, contributing their unique cadence to the grand cosmic symphony and reinforcing the decentralized governance principle.

Think of vibrational energies as different genres of music. Each genre evokes a distinct emotional response – classical music might bring a sense of calm, while rock might energize you. Similarly, different vibrational energies influence our mood and perspective. Higher vibrational energies, like a harmonious symphony, can uplift and inspire us, leading to feelings of joy and peace. In contrast, lower vibrational energies, akin to a discordant sound, might correspond to feelings of sadness or anxiety. Our personal universe 'resonates' with these energies, affecting our emotional and mental state.

The personal universes (such as Humans) vibrating at frequencies akin to our own come closer in this intricate web, having a more immediate and discernible impact on our personal reality. Conversely, those oscillators (personal universes) that hum at a vastly different pitch - representing states of being far removed from our own - might as well be distant stars in the cosmic fabric. Their influence is minimal, and their presence is barely felt. Yet, no part of the web operates in isolation; the slightest vibration, no matter how distant, contributes to the collective resonance.

Decentralized governance in the cosmos, as in our personal universes, presents a blueprint for harmonious coexistence. It emphasizes the role of each quantum oscillator - every thought, every feeling, every act of creation - and acknowledges the profound effect of those vibrating with intensity, whether from love or despair. By understanding and embracing this model, we can navigate toward life in sync with the broader cosmic order, fostering a harmonious, balanced existence attuned to the greater symphony of life. Have you wondered about the poems and pictures in this book? Now you may understand why we have them.

In the cosmic dance, a governance so fine,
Decentralized, resonating, in quantum design.
Every entity, a note in the divine concerto,
Influences, and is influenced by, the grand stiletto.

Personal universes, oscillations in space,
Vibrate higher frequencies, in this cosmic embrace.
Love, compassion, gratitude, the rhythm of our lives,
Shape the quantum field, where each note thrives.

Art and music, beauty, rituals divine,
Echo quantum oscillations, in governance design.
Resonating with consciousness, evoking deep emotion,
Ripple through the quantum field, a cosmic ocean.

Chapter 9:
The Etheric Field, Akashic Records, and the Transpersonal Space

"The cosmos is within us. We are made of star-stuff. We are a way for the universe to know itself."

- Carl Sagan

Understanding Ether:
The Quintessence of the Multiverse

As we delve deeper into the dance of the Karmic Multiverse, we delve into the mystical realms of the Etheric Field and the Akashic Records, which serve as bridges between our physical world and spiritual dimensions. Imagine the Etheric Field as an all-encompassing ocean, not of water, but of a fine, ethereal substance. This ocean, much like water, is a medium of memory and connection, invisibly linking all life forms. It's akin to the air around us - ever-present, vital, yet unseen. The Akashic Records, in this context, resemble an infinite, cosmic library, submerged within this etheric ocean. Here, the memories of every soul, the history of the cosmos, and the potentialities of future events are meticulously archived. Like a vast database, it holds the records of the past, the unfolding present, and the myriad possibilities of the future. By visualizing these profound concepts as parts of an immense, memory-rich ocean, we can better understand their importance and their impact on the intricate weave of our personal experiences and the broader universe.

Ether, known as "Akasha" in Hindu philosophy and deemed the fifth element by Ancient Greeks, is often described as the invisible fabric of the universe, a field of potentiality from which all physical reality manifests. It's said to be the medium through which consciousness expresses itself, and through which we, as conscious beings, interact with the greater multiverse.

Modern science, too, has grappled with the concept of Ether. Once postulated as the medium for the propagation of light in space, the 'luminiferous Ether' was later discarded with the advent of Einstein's theory of relativity. However, with the development of quantum field theory, a new perspective of Ether has emerged - one that aligns more closely with its spiritual interpretation.

Understanding Ether can deepen our insights into the nature of consciousness and our place within the karmic multiverse. It can help us realize how our Intentions, thoughts, emotions, and actions ripple through this etheric field, influencing our personal universe and the multiverse at large.

Accessing the Akashic Records for Personal Growth and Understanding

The Akashic Records, a term coined in theosophy and anthroposophy, refer to a compendium of all human events, thoughts, words, emotions, and intent ever to have occurred in the past, present, or future. They are encoded in the astral plane, or the etheric field, and are accessible through certain states of consciousness. Accessing the Akashic Records can provide profound insights into our past lives, our soul's journey, and our karmic imprints. It can guide our spiritual growth, help resolve past traumas, and illuminate our path forward. Moreover, the Akashic Records can deepen our understanding of the interconnectedness of all beings, enriching our dance within the karmic multiverse.

The Unified Field: A Quantum Melody

Modern science talks about the Unified Field, a singular, all-encompassing field from which all particles and fundamental forces - gravity, electromagnetism, and the strong and weak nuclear forces - arise. This Unified Field serves as the underlying fabric of the universe, the source of all matter and energy, and the foundation of all forms and phenomena.

The Unified Field is not merely a collection of individual, separate entities, but a cohesive, interconnected whole. Every particle, every force, and every bit of matter or energy is, in essence, a localized expression of this field. What we perceive as separate entities interacting are, in fact, excitations of the Unified Field interacting with each other.

This understanding of the Unified Field brings forth a profound sense of interconnectedness. It is in this field that the roots of phenomena such as quantum entanglement lie. We, along with everything in the universe, are deeply interconnected manifestations of the Unified Field. Recognizing this interconnectedness can inspire a deeper awareness of our place in the cosmos and the impact of our actions.

Exploring the Transpersonal Space: A Journey Beyond the Self

Venturing beyond the Etheric Field and the Akashic Records, we find ourselves at the threshold of the Transpersonal Space. This dimension of consciousness extends beyond the personal self, interweaving the minds of all beings in a cosmic dance of interconnectedness.

The Transpersonal Space is not a physical domain but a realm of consciousness. It is the space where our individual consciousness merges with the collective, enabling us to partake in a shared dance within the karmic multiverse. This space is the realm of collective unconsciousness, the home of archetypal patterns, shared spiritual experiences, and universal truths.

Accessing the Transpersonal Space is an active process, requiring intentional expansion of our consciousness. It involves practices such as deep meditation, holotropic breathwork, mindfulness, and various forms of transpersonal psychology. As we align ourselves with this realm, we begin to perceive the interconnected dance of all existence and become aware of the collective karmic imprints that shape the multiverse.

In the Transpersonal Space, we witness the ripple effects of our actions on a cosmic scale. We understand that our dance within our personal universe influences the entire multiverse. As we navigate this space, we become conscious participants in the cosmic resonance, adding our unique notes to the grand symphony of the karmic multiverse. Reflect on a moment in your life where you felt deeply connected to something greater than yourself. How does the concept of the Etheric Field as the invisible fabric of the universe help you understand or reinterpret this experience?

In the unseen realm of the starry sky,
Lies the Ether, the Akasha, where dreams and reality lie.
A field of endless possibilities, where thoughts and matter blend,
Each thought a ripple, each dream a message to send.

Within this etheric field, a book of life exists,
The Akashic Records, where our life stories persist.
Past, present, and future, in a timeless dance unite,
Echoing each moment of our journey, day and night.

Beyond the Ether and Akasha, a broader realm unfolds,
The Transpersonal Space, where shared consciousness holds.
Here, we're all connected, individuality is set free,
Each soul a note in the cosmic song, part of a harmonious spree.

As we journey deeper into this book, please remember: I'm here not as a teacher, but as a fellow traveler. My goal isn't instruction, but liberation and empowerment; and if you feel triggered, I invite you to read the book foreword again.

In this grand dance of life, we are both choreographers and co-creators shaping our destinies. **We stand on equal footing, each with the power to architect our lives.** With humility and camaraderie, I invite you to join us embracing this power, unfolding our creative potential, and stepping confidently into the dance of destiny.

Disclaimer for Advanced Practices

This book contains discussions of advanced practices, including but not limited to meditation, yogic sadhana, breathwork, astral projection, and the use of entheogens. These practices can have powerful psychological and physiological effects and should not be undertaken without appropriate preparation and guidance. **Do not engage in the very advanced spiritual practices without prior cultivation of abiding inner silence!**

The author and publisher strongly advise that anyone wishing to engage in these practices seek the advice of competent professionals and ensure that they are acting in accordance with all applicable laws and regulations. It is the reader's responsibility to research the health and legal implications of any practices mentioned in this book.

The author and publisher disclaim any liability for any adverse effects arising from the use or application of the information contained herein. The inclusion of these practices in the book is not a recommendation for anyone to perform them without professional guidance or prior experience.

Chapter 10:
Advanced Techniques for Personal Universe Mastery

"Mastering others is strength. Mastering oneself makes you fearless."

- Lao Tzu

Rituals for Alignment

As we become more adept at navigating our personal universe, we can begin to explore advanced techniques that further heighten our awareness, expand our consciousness, and harmonize our dance within the karmic multiverse. These practices, drawn from various spiritual traditions and pioneering scientific theories, can provide us with powerful tools for personal universe mastery.

Mindfulness Practices from East and West

Mindfulness, the act of being fully present and engaged in the current moment, serves as the cornerstone of this alignment. From the Buddhist practice of Vipassana to the Sufi concept of Muraqaba, or vigilant self-observation, the essence of mindfulness permeates diverse spiritual traditions.

Starting each day with a moment of mindfulness can anchor us in the present, allowing clarity and tranquility to seep into our day. This simple act of conscious presence can serve as a protective shield, enabling us to navigate the day with serenity and purpose. In this practice of daily mindfulness, we embody the highest form of intelligence: observing without judgment. By cultivating an attitude of non-judgmental awareness, we open ourselves to experience life more fully, without the constraints of preconceived notions or biases. This approach not only enriches our understanding of the world around us but also fosters a deeper connection with our inner selves. As we move through our day, this mindful observation becomes a tool of insight and calmness, guiding us through life's complexities with a composed and discerning heart. Through this practice, we learn to embrace each moment as it unfolds, finding wisdom in simplicity and strength in stillness.

Meditation: The Path to Receptive Stillness

In the art of meditation, the key to quieting the mind lies in developing equanimity toward our thoughts and sensations. By observing our mental chatter with a balanced, non-reactive attitude, we gradually shift from a state of constant 'sending' - talking, thinking, praying, acting - to one of 'receiving'. In this stillness, where the mind no longer dominates with its noise, we open ourselves to the subtle, often missed responses of the universe. It is in this silence that we can truly receive, be it intuitive insights or answers to our innermost questions, allowing the universe's wisdom to flow into our conscious awareness.

Nature's Wisdom: Shamanic Practices and Modern Science

Nature, with its rhythms and cycles, is a vibrant reflection of the multiverse. Shamanic traditions across the globe recognize nature as a potent healer and teacher. By attuning ourselves to its rhythms, we can heal, rejuvenate, and align our personal universe with the multiverse.

Modern science echoes this ancient wisdom, with studies demonstrating the therapeutic effects of nature on our physical and mental well-being. Spending time outdoors, whether it's a walk in the park, tending to a garden, or simply sitting under the stars, can rejuvenate our spirit and align us with the rhythms of the cosmos.

Building a Spiritual Community: Shared Experiences and Collective Growth

Every journey becomes richer when shared, and our voyage through the multiverse is no exception. Building a spiritual community can offer companionship, shared wisdom, and collective growth. From the Yogic concept of Satsang, a gathering of truth-seekers, to the Sufi practice of Sohbet, a spiritual conversation, the importance of communal support and learning is acknowledged in diverse spiritual traditions.

By engaging in meaningful conversations, sharing silences, and collectively exploring the realms of the multiverse, we can weave a tapestry of shared experiences and insights, enriching our personal and collective journey.

Astral Travel and Remote Viewing: Exploring Beyond the Physical

Beyond the tangible reality perceived by our senses lies a realm of infinite possibilities. Practices like astral travel, also known as "soul travel" in some esoteric traditions, allow the consciousness to journey beyond the confines of the physical body, exploring ethereal realms and gaining insights into the deeper mysteries of existence.

Similarly, remote viewing, a practice that involves perceiving a target - place, person, object - that is hidden from physical view, can expand our perceptual boundaries and enhance our understanding of the interconnectedness of the multiverse.

These practices, while requiring training and discipline, can deepen our understanding of our personal universe and its dance within the grand multiverse, providing us with unique perspectives and insights.

Entheogens, Consciousness Expansion, Deconstructing, and Root Healing:

Entheogens, sacred plant medicines used in spiritual or shamanic practices, can guide us to tap into the energies of the multiverse. When used responsibly and respectfully, entheogens can facilitate profound spiritual experiences, providing insights into the nature of self and the universe by expanding our consciousness and dissolving and transcending our ego. Their profound ability to expand consciousness offers more than just a glimpse into the multiverse; they serve as potent catalysts for the deconstruction of our deeply ingrained often distorted perceptions. This sacred process begins with the unraveling of the mind, ego, self, and the very fabric of what we perceive as reality.

The Unraveling of the Ego and the Mind: Under the gentle guidance of these plant medicines, the rigid structures of the ego begin to dissolve. This dissolution paves the way for a deeper, more honest introspection. The mind, often cluttered with incessant thoughts and societal conditioning, finds itself in a state of unprecedented clarity. In this space, the barriers between the self and the universe start to blur, leading to profound realizations about our interconnectedness with all that exists.

Beyond the Self – The Expansion into Multiversal Energies: As the ego diminishes, the self expands into realms previously unimagined. We become attuned to the subtle energies of the multiverse, engaging in a dialogue that transcends words. This expansion is not just a journey outward into the cosmos, but also inward, into the depths of our soul. It's here, in the sanctity of this inner cosmos, that we begin to see the illusionary nature of our perceived reality.

The Return Journey – Reverse Engineering Reality: The journey with entheogens, however, is not complete with the mere experience of dissolution and expansion. The true essence of this journey lies in the return. As we gently re-emerge into our usual state of consciousness, we carry with us the imprints of these profound experiences. It is in this phase that the significant, life-changing personal learning takes place.

Armed with new perspectives, we begin the intricate process of reverse engineering our reality. This involves reassembling our experiences, insights, and revelations to reconstruct a reality that is more aligned with our newfound understanding. This reconstructed reality is richer, more vibrant, and deeply connected to the universal truths we glimpsed during our entheogenic journey.

Integration – The Path to Transformation: The integration of these experiences into our daily lives marks the beginning of the true transformation. The insights gained are not just philosophical musings but root healing and practical wisdom that can guide our actions, decisions, and interactions. This process of integration is where the seeds of spiritual growth are nurtured, leading to a more conscious, mindful, and fulfilling existence.

While these practices can offer deep insights, it's crucial to approach them wisely, with respect, preparation, and, optimally, with the guidance of an experienced practitioner. It's also important to consider legal implications and to ensure that the use of entheogens is in alignment with one's personal values and spiritual path.

Sacred Geometry:
Decoding the Blueprint of the Multiverse

Sacred geometry refers to geometric patterns and shapes that have deep spiritual and symbolic meanings. From the Sri Yantra in Indian Tantric traditions to the Flower of Life found in various ancient cultures, sacred geometry offers a blueprint for understanding the fundamental structure of the multiverse and aligning with it.

In sacred geometry, fractals represent an iterative process where a pattern repeats, regardless of the scale at which you view it. They symbolize the infinite nature of the cosmos and the endless dance of creation and dissolution. In the quantum realm, similar recursive processes are evident, where subatomic particles form atoms, atoms form molecules, molecules form cells, and so forth. Each level is a reflection of the patterns that came before, hinting at the recursive nature of reality. In the context of karma, this suggests that our intentions, thoughts, and emotions have reverberating consequences, rippling through our personal universe in endless cycles of cause and effect. A profound way to directly experience these sacred patterns is through entheogens or holotropic breathwork.

Holotropic Breathwork: Accessing Non-Ordinary
States of Consciousness

Holotropic Breathwork is a transformative practice developed to access expanded states of consciousness through the natural rhythm of the breath. Combining accelerated breathing with evocative music in a safe, contained setting, this method allows practitioners to journey beyond the ordinary mind and tap into the deeper layers of the psyche. Often accompanied by spontaneous insights, emotional release, and profound spiritual experiences, Holotropic Breathwork can illuminate unconscious patterns and bring about deep inner healing. When practiced with clear intention and integration, it becomes a powerful tool for exploring and harmonizing the vast inner landscape - enabling one to navigate the karmic multiverse with greater clarity, presence, and authenticity.

Awareness Through the Body (ATB): Integrating Subtle Realms of Existence

Awareness Through the Body (ATB) is an advanced practice deeply rooted in the principles of Integral Yoga. It facilitates a refined exploration of self-awareness and subtle consciousness. Practitioners engage in structured exercises aimed at enhancing sustained attention, sensory perception, and mindful presence, allowing direct experience of various dimensions of their being - such as the subtle physical, vital, and mental bodies. Through this integrated practice, individuals cultivate the capacity to consciously navigate and master the different planes of their personal universe, aligning their inner realms harmoniously within the expansive dance of the karmic multiverse.

In the dance of stars and the cosmic tide,
Advanced techniques for mastery we confide.
Through ritual and nature, we align,
In our personal universe, divine designs shine.

Awake in mindfulness, we start our day,
In silence and presence, find our way.
Embrace the wisdom that nature imparts,
Its rhythms and cycles, healing arts.

In a community of souls, we weave,
Shared wisdom, collective truths, we achieve.
In this grand dance, we find our place,
In the karmic multiverse, we embrace grace.

Chapter 11:
Beyond Body and Mind: Embracing the True Self

"What you are looking for is what is looking"

- St Francis of Assisi

The Illusion of Identity

We tend to identify ourselves with our physical body and our mind. Thoughts, emotions, and sensory experiences shape our perception of who we are. However, spiritual traditions and contemporary consciousness research suggest that our essence extends beyond these physical and mental constructs.

Our cultural, societal, and personal narratives often bind us to the belief that we are our bodies and minds. The physical body, with its sensory experiences and visible presence, offers a tangible identity. Similarly, our thoughts, emotions, and memories form a mental identity, constructing the narrative of "I". Yet, this identification presents a limited perspective of our True Self.

The Body as a Community

In our exploration of self-identity and the physical body, we encounter a fascinating perspective: our body as a complex community. This idea can be more easily grasped if we think of our body not just as a single entity, but as a bustling city teeming with life. Within this city, countless residents – bacteria, fungi, viruses, and other microorganisms, collectively known as the microbiome – live in harmony. Intriguingly, these non-human cells outnumber our human cells, presenting a thought-provoking question about our identity. Are we simply the sum of our individual cells, or are we more accurately the stewards of this diverse and thriving metropolis?

The Elected Representatives of Our Bodies

If we imagine ourselves as the elected representatives of this incredibly diverse community of life forms that constitute our body. We do not own our bodies in the traditional sense, but rather, we are caretakers, responsible for maintaining the harmony and balance within this complex ecosystem. This perspective shifts our relationship with our body from one of ownership to one of stewardship, reflecting a more holistic and interconnected notion of identity.

Beyond the Physical and Mental

Within us exists an essence unaffected by the body's aging or the mind's fluctuations. This consciousness, the observer of our experiences, remains constant. It is the silent witness to our thoughts and emotions, the entity that experiences the sensations of the physical body.

Hindu philosophy refers to this as the "Atman" or the True Self, while in Buddhist teachings, it aligns with the concept of "Buddha-nature." Contemporary consciousness studies also point toward this deeper level of identity, suggesting that consciousness is fundamental to reality.

Embracing the True Self

Recognizing ourselves as more than just our body and mind can be a liberating experience. It invites us to connect with the constant, unchanging aspect of ourselves, which remains unperturbed by life's ups and downs. This can lead to immense peace, equanimity, and a deeper understanding of our place in the multiverse.

Meditation and mindfulness practices can facilitate this understanding. By quieting the mind and tuning into our inner observer, we can begin to experience our True Self. We can realize that while we have a body and a mind, we are not exclusively these entities.

While our bodies, minds, and egos are integral aspects of our human experience, they can never define us entirely. By acknowledging and connecting with our True Self, and recognizing our role as stewards of our bodies, we can experience life in its fullest dimension, enrich our journey through the multiverse, and move toward our desired reality. Reflect on a moment when you felt that you were more than just your body and mind. What sparked this realization, and how did it make you feel?

In this vessel we dwell, a cosmos within,
A myriad life forms beneath the skin,
Human and non-human in a dance entwined,
A symphony of existence, rhythm divine.

Elected we are, stewards of this sea,
Our bodies are ours, yet not solely 'me'.
We're the mindful caretakers on a cosmic journey,
Guiding this ship through life's stormy tourney.

Beyond flesh and thought, a beacon resides,
An eternal observer where True Self abides,
A silent witness amidst life's ceaseless roars,
Unchanging, unending, forever it endures.

Chapter 12:
Ego - The Dance of Identity in the Karmic Multiverse

"Give up the ego but not the self."

- Ramana Maharshi

The Ego: Friend or Foe?

The ego, often depicted as an adversary in spiritual discourse, is an integral part of our psychological makeup. It shapes our sense of self, enables us to navigate the physical world, and serves as a protective shield in challenging situations. Thus, the ego is not a foe to be vanquished, but a component of our consciousness to be understood and recognized as our servant or rather as a partner.

In our dance within the Karmic Multiverse, the ego plays a unique role. It allows us to experience individuality within the cosmic unity, engage with the physical world, and learn from our unique journey. However, when the ego becomes overly dominant, it can lead us to feel separate from the multiverse, creating illusions of isolation and competition.

Ego and Karma: The Interplay of Action and Identity Toward Unity

The ego is closely intertwined with the concept of Karma. Our actions, driven by our ego identities, contribute to our karmic imprints, shaping our personal universe and our journey through the Karmic Multiverse. By comprehending the dynamic relationship between ego and karma, we can steer our journey through the cosmos with heightened consciousness and insight.

Transcending the ego does not mean annihilating it, but rather balancing our individuality with our inherent unity with the multiverse. This involves acknowledging the ego's role, understanding its limitations, and cultivating a broader sense of identity that encompasses both our individual self and our interconnectedness with all existence.

Practical Techniques for Ego Transcendence

Techniques for transcending the ego can range from mindfulness and meditation practices that cultivate present-moment awareness, over breathwork or entheogenic shamanic sacred medicine, to self-inquiry methods that probe into the nature of the self. These practices can help us navigate the play of the ego, transforming it from a potential stumbling block into a stepping stone toward deeper self-understanding and cosmic resonance.

In the grand theater of cosmic dance,
A player takes the stage, bold and askance,
The Ego, its name, a dance of its own,
In the Karmic Multiverse, its seeds are sown.

A friend or a foe, in the dance so grand?
A question posed on shifting sand.
Not a foe to be vanquished, but a role to learn,
In the cosmic choreography, a twist and turn.

Transcending the ego, the dance elevates,
From individuality to unity, the dancer resonates.
A cosmic dance of interconnected glee,
In the Karmic Multiverse, the Ego is free.

Chapter 13:
The Shadow Dance - Unveiling the Hidden Self

*"Until you make the unconscious conscious,
it will direct your life and you will call it fate."*

- Carl Jung

The Shadow: The Unseen Dance Partner

As we continue our exploration of the cosmic dance within the Karmic Multiverse, we plunge into the realm of our own hidden self - the Shadow. Coined by psychiatrist Carl Jung, the Shadow represents the unconscious aspects of our personality that we disown or reject. These can include traits, emotions, and desires that we deem unacceptable or inappropriate. While these aspects might remain hidden in our daily dance, they subtly influence our intentions, thoughts, emotions, and actions, and thus, our personal universe.

The Shadow, with its unacknowledged desires and suppressed emotions, can heavily influence our karmic imprints. Actions driven by unrecognized shadow aspects can lead to karmic patterns that we struggle to understand or change. Recognizing, acknowledging, and integrating our Shadow is thus crucial for a harmonious dance within the Karmic Multiverse.

The Dance of Integration: Embracing Light and Dark

The ultimate aim of shadow work is not to eliminate the Shadow, but to integrate it. This means acknowledging and engaging with our Shadow aspects only when they surface, directing our energy toward them with the light of unconditional love at those moments. This conscious direction of loving attention and energy facilitates healing and integration of the Shadow, without continuously nourishing it with our focus. As we align our attention with positive transformation, we amplify growth, allowing the Shadow to become a supportive force in our upward spiral of evolution.

Our Shadow, despite its name, is not to be feared or rejected. It is an integral part of our cosmic dance - a dance partner with whom we must learn to move in harmony. By embracing and integrating our Shadow, we can enrich our dance, deepen our self-understanding, and enhance our resonance within the Karmic Multiverse.

The journey into the Shadow also leads us into silence and emptiness - the sacred void where transformation begins. If we wish to find the light, we must first enter the darkness. As visualized in the ancient symbol of Yin and Yang, it is within the heart of darkness that a seed of light resides. And equally, within the heart of light lies a speck of darkness. This is not a mere poetic metaphor - it is a metaphysical truth. The reality we perceive is, in many ways, a luminous trap: if you seek the light in the light alone, you will only find a deeper shadow at its core. That is the secret of yin and yang - the revelation that only by embracing both can we access the wholeness of being.

With this deeper understanding, let us continue our healing journey - entering the silence, embracing the emptiness, and integrating the hidden truths that reality conceals. In doing so, we awaken to a more complete, more sovereign existence, weaving the full spectrum of our humanity into the vast choreography of the Karmic Multiverse. And as we walk this path, may we hold with reverence the creative tension between light and emptiness, masculine and feminine, form and formlessness, order and chaos - for it is through this sacred polarity that consciousness evolves, and life itself is birthed within the sacred embrace of Trinity.

In the cosmic dance, beneath the radiant self,
Lies a Shadow, unseen, a clandestine wealth.
Rejected, ignored, yet swaying unseen,
In the dance of the Karmic Multiverse, a hidden scene.

Unseen it may be, its influence profound,
In the karmic echoes, its whispers resound.
To acknowledge its presence, a courageous task,
In the cosmic spotlight, the Shadow we unmask.

Shadow work, a dance of the soul,
Illuminating the dark, making us whole.
In the dance of integration, the shadow embraced,
In the Karmic Multiverse, no part is misplaced.

You've now woven through the chapters of cosmic interplay and quantum entanglement, discovering the symphony of decentralized governance and the resonant web of the universe.

In view of all this and the immense sacred power you hold, the question arises: 'What now?'

Embrace the power you have, the intricate dance of energies you're a part of, and consider the pathways opening up to you. What intentions will you set? How will you use your unique rhythm to influence the grand choreography of existence?

Take a moment, **breathe** in the potential, and as you exhale, step forward into the realm of action with purpose and passion ♡

Chapter 14:
Unity and Healing: A Shamanic Perspective and the Role of Yoga

"Yoga is the journey of the self, through the self, to the self."

- The Bhagavad Gita

The Illusion of Separation: A Cosmic Sickness

As we surf the quantum waves of the multiverse, carving a path through nebulous opaque chaos of endless probabilities, an essential principle emerges from the mist of cosmic understanding - the shamanic saying: "Separation is the sickness, unity is the healing."

The concept of separation can be seen as a cosmic sickness. It is the erroneous perception that we are distinct and isolated entities, separate from the rest of the universe. This mindset is not only inaccurate, given the interconnected nature of all things at the quantum level, but it also breeds disharmony and conflict. It disrupts our personal universe and hinders our fluid connection within the karmic multiverse, creating dissonance in the cosmic symphony.

Unity: The Path to Healing

The antidote to this sickness is unity. Recognizing that we are all interwoven parts of a grand cosmic tapestry is the first step toward healing. Unity does not imply uniformity but acknowledges diversity within a greater whole. It is the understanding that every rhythm, however unique, contributes to the grand cosmic dance. Once we embrace this principle, we can align our frequency with the universe. In the next sections, we will explore ways to achieve this harmonious resonance.

Yoga: A Pathway to Unity

The term 'Yoga' originates from the Sanskrit word 'yuj', which means to yoke or unify. Yoga is an ancient practice that aims to create a balance between body, mind, energies, and spirit, promoting a sense of unity within oneself and with the universe. Yoga practices allow us to experience our interconnectedness and unity with the cosmos.

Shamanic Practices for Unity and Healing

Shamanic traditions across the globe emphasize the healing power of unity. They offer various practices to dissolve the illusion of separation and foster a sense of interconnectedness. These include rituals, meditations, drumming to synchronize the heartbeat, and the use of entheogens in controlled, respectful settings. Such practices encourage us to experience our fundamental unity with all things, thereby promoting healing and wholeness.

Unity in the Karmic Multiverse

In the context of the Karmic Multiverse, the principle of unity takes on an even deeper significance. Each thought, intention, emotion, and action, ripples out into the multiverse, influencing and being influenced by the grand cosmic web. By dissolving the sense of separation and embracing unity, we can contribute to a harmonious multiverse, healing not only ourselves but also influencing the entire cosmic dance in a positive manner. The journey from separation to unity, thus, is not only a journey of personal healing but also a journey of cosmic harmony. Have you experienced a sense of unity or healing through any spiritual or physical practice, like yoga, breathwork or shamanic rituals? How do these practices contribute to your sense of connectedness with yourself and the universe?

Quantum pulses guide our radiant flight,
In personal universes, we kindle insight.
Yoga's wisdom, breath's gentle flow,
Reconnect us deeply to truths we know.

Separation fades, a mere cosmic disguise,
In unity's embrace, true healing lies.
Shamanic whispers, sacred and clear,
Remind us: our wholeness is already here.

Through conscious practice, our hearts expand,
Joining the symphony, hand in hand.
Together, harmonizing the cosmic song,
Healing ourselves, and where we belong.

Chapter 15:
Integral Yoga, Karma Yoga, Love, Compassion, and Gratitude

"The individual is indeed the key to the evolutionary movement; for it is the individual who finds himself, who becomes conscious of the Reality."

- Sri Aurobindo

Integral Yoga: Unity in Diversity

Through our existence, one is invited to experience the profound truth of Oneness. This inherent unity is palpable in every breath, every moment, and every action. Herein lies the exploration of Integral Yoga and Karma Yoga, woven with the golden threads of love, compassion, and gratitude, all serving as a gentle reminder of the Oneness within the personal universe.

Integral Yoga presents a comprehensive framework that integrates every facet of existence into a unified whole, fostering a profound sense of oneness with the cosmos and the Supermind. It is not limited to physical practices but envelops the full spectrum of life - mental, emotional, physical, spiritual, and community living. This system advocates for each thought, each deed, and every moment of life to be imbued with spiritual significance, transforming daily experiences into acts of conscious evolution. In this holistic practice, the mundane becomes sacred, and every aspect of life is harmonized into a seamless expression of divine unity, allowing individuals to live in alignment with the cosmic rhythm, where the personal and universal become indistinguishable.

Through the lens of Yoga, the universe is not an assembly of separate entities but a unified field of consciousness. The perceived separations are mere illusions, born of conventional perspectives. As the practice of Integral Yoga deepens, the grand cosmic dance of unity in diversity becomes evident, revealing that each personal universe is an integral part of the grand cosmic orchestra.

Karma Yoga: The Yoga of Action

Karma Yoga, the yoga of action, is a path that illuminates this unity. It is the practice of selfless action, offering deeds to the greater good, devoid of any attachment to the outcome. Each action, performed with this consciousness, becomes a sacred offering to the cosmic rhythm.

The understanding that every other being is but a reflection of oneself naturally leads actions to flow from a place of love and compassion. Karma Yoga thus becomes a powerful tool to navigate the personal universe, aligning every action with the cosmic dance of the multiverse.

Love, Compassion, and Gratitude: The Harmonic Melodies

Love, compassion, and gratitude are not mere emotions. They are harmonic melodies orchestrating the cosmic dance. These are universal frequencies resonating with the rhythm of the multiverse.

Love is the fundamental force that binds everything together. When actions stem from love, the personal universe aligns with the grand symphony of the multiverse.

Compassion, the capacity to empathize with others, emerges from the realization of shared existence. It is understanding that the other is not separate but a part of oneself. Compassion allows for dancing in harmony with the cosmic rhythm with each step echoing understanding and empathy.

Gratitude, a heartfelt appreciation for blessings, is a potent force that amplifies cosmic resonance. It is the acknowledgment of interconnectedness, the recognition of the grand cosmic dance unfolding in every moment.

In the resonance of love, compassion, and gratitude, we find not just a passive alignment with the universe, but an active influence upon it. These highest frequencies, being closest to the Source, are powerful conduits through which we shape the cosmic fabric. When we vibrate at these elevated levels, we engage in Quantum Oscillation Synchronization, the dynamic process where our individual energy patterns don't just align, but actively contribute to the universal rhythm. This means that our expressions of love, compassion, and gratitude extend beyond personal transformation; they send ripples across the multiverse, influencing its very essence. We are not mere participants in the cosmic dance but co-creators, whose frequencies have the power to alter the universal melody. By resonating with these purest forms of energy, we assert a profound impact on the cosmic order, affirming our role as integral architects of the universe's ongoing evolution.

Weaving the Dance of Oneness

As the practice of Integral Yoga and Karma Yoga deepens, infused with the melodies of love, compassion, and gratitude; harmony with the cosmic rhythm is found. The personal universe begins to resonate with the grand multiverse, and the profound truth of Oneness is experienced.

In this dance, there is no separation between 'I' and 'the other'. The realization begins to dawn that the cosmic dance isn't happening 'out there', but is unfolding within, through, and as oneself.

In the cosmic dance of unity we twirl,
Where Karma and Integral Yoga unfurl.
A weave of Love, Compassion, Gratitude in sight,
In this grand ballet of cosmic light.

A symphony of existence resonates deep,
Where Self and Other no longer sleep.
In the dance, the dancers are but one,
A universe's tale being spun.

So dance, oh soul, in this cosmic play,
Know in each other, ourselves we display.
In the grand ballet of the cosmos, take part,
For in every dance, we touch a single heart.

Chapter 16:
The Cosmic Dance of Unconditional Love

"The day the power of love overrules the love of power, the world will know peace."

- Mahatma Gandhi

Unconditional Love: The Heartbeat of the Cosmos

In the grand design of the cosmos, one theme resonates with profound clarity as an all-encompassing, transcendent, and transformative force. This force is none other than Unconditional Love, a sublime melody that orchestrates the cosmic dance.

Unconditional Love serves as the heartbeat in the cosmic symphony, a rhythm so fundamental to existence that its sheer magnitude and significance often remain overlooked. This energy transcends the boundaries of the ego, the confines of the physical, and the limitations of the mind, reverberating through every corner of the multiverse.

Transcending the realm of emotions and affections, Unconditional Love emerges as a state of being as an all-encompassing acceptance that perceives beyond flaws, shortcomings, and transgressions. It is an embracing of all that is, with an open heart and a tranquil mind. It's the understanding of the inherent divinity in all forms of existence. Unconditional Love is thus the conscious embrace of the interconnected dance of the cosmos.

The Dance of Unconditional Love

Unconditional Love is not merely a passive acceptance but an active engagement with the world. It is a dance, a harmonious movement that aligns the personal universe with the multiverse. This dance invites participation in the cosmic choreography, where every particle, every wave, and every entity swirls in a harmonious ballet.

Unconditional Love allows a perception beyond the illusion of separation and urges an experience of union beyond the boundaries of "I" and "the other". It prompts a recognition of the divine in all, thereby dissolving the illusion of duality and revealing the unity of existence.

Unconditional Love and Karmic Evolution

In the realm of Karma, Unconditional Love holds an esteemed place. It is the energy that propels toward karmic evolution, guiding from a state of fragmentation to a state of unity, from a state of conflict to a state of harmony.

Sending out waves of Unconditional Love contributes to the harmonious resonance of the multiverse. These waves of love, like ripples spreading across a cosmic ocean, influence the dance of the cosmos. The more alignment exists with the energy of Unconditional Love, the more alignment of the personal universe manifests with the multiverse. This alignment accelerates karmic evolution, guiding toward the realization of the true self.

Mastering the Dance of Unconditional Love

Mastering the dance of Unconditional Love is a journey, not a destination. It involves constant self-awareness, self-inquiry, and self-transcendence. Here are some practical steps to facilitate this journey:

- **Practicing Compassion:** Compassion is the first step toward Unconditional Love. It is a humble acknowledgment of the shared human condition. Compassion invites understanding and empathy with the joys, sorrows, struggles, and triumphs of all beings.

- **Cultivating Self-Love:** To love others unconditionally, self-love is what must be cultivated first. This involves accepting strengths, weaknesses, achievements, and mistakes with an open heart. It requires embracing the journey, with all its twists and turns, as an essential part of growth.

- **Practicing Forgiveness:** Unconditional Love is incomplete without forgiveness. Forgiveness enables us to let go of resentment and anger, thus freeing us to experience and share Unconditional Love more fully.

- **Living Mindfully:** Mindfulness allows us to stay present, to experience life as it unfolds, and to respond with Unconditional Love. It helps to see the interconnectedness of all things, reinforcing the practice of Unconditional Love.

- **Meditating on Love:** Meditation can be a powerful tool to cultivate Unconditional Love. Meditating on love can help tap into this profound energy, allowing it to permeate the being and radiate outwards.

Unconditional Love is the very cosmic dance that weaves all together. This profound force, when embraced, has the potential to transform the personal universe and contribute to the harmonious resonance of the multiverse. Considering Unconditional Love as the "heartbeat of the cosmos," how might you cultivate a state of being that embodies this all-encompassing acceptance in your daily interactions, even in situations where flaws and transgressions are evident?

A rhythm emerges, potent and bold,
In the grand cosmic ballet, a story told.
Unconditional Love, transcending the physical sphere,
Echoes in existence, both far and near.

A state of being, acceptance profound,
In all of existence, its echoes are found.
In divinity's dance, it weaves and it twines,
Uniting the cosmos in harmonious lines.

Active engagement, not mere passive care,
A dance with the universe, an invitation to share.
Beyond the illusion of "I" and "the other",
It sees the divine in each sister and brother.

Chapter 17:
The Source: Unconditional Love, Self-Love, and the Heart's Resonance

"Love is the most powerful force in the world. If people tell you that the opposite of love is fear, it is not so. Love just is. Love has no opposite. Remember that, dear one. Love has no opposite. Love just is. It is the answer to everything. Everything."

- Dolores Cannon

The Source: Heart of the Universe

As we traverse the cosmic fabric of existence, which at times feels like a labyrinth because we are not constantly aware of its intelligent structure, our quest leads us to an age-old question contemplated by philosophers, scientists, and truth seekers for centuries: What is the Source? Whether we envision it as the singularity, the divine, or the fundamental energy permeating all existence, the Source signifies the beginning and the end, the alpha and omega of everything.

When we shift our perspective inward, we discover the Source in the most intimate and profound place: our hearts, the spiritual heart. It sits in the center of our chest, is the emotional and spiritual epicenter of our being, and is the wellspring of unconditional love. This love, free from judgment and expectations, is the purest manifestation of our authentic nature. This vibrational frequency connects us to all of existence, echoing the resonant hum of the Source within us.

Self-Love: The Key to Conscious Co-Creation

In our journey toward becoming conscious co-creators, self-love emerges as a crucial key. It is in loving ourselves unconditionally, accepting our strengths and weaknesses, and honoring our unique journeys that we unlock our true potential. This act of opening our hearts to ourselves, of truly embracing who we are, can be one of the most transformative experiences in our lives. We will discuss this in more detail in the following chapters.

The Source, when perceived from this heart-centered perspective, can be likened to the conductor of a grand symphony of love. From the smallest quantum strings to the largest galaxies, all are part of this harmonious concert, each playing their part, each contributing to the melody of existence. The Source, the heart, sets the rhythm and pace, guiding the dance of existence with the steady beat of unconditional love. In what ways can you tune into your heart's resonance more deeply to access this wellspring of unconditional love, and how might this practice transform your perception of self and others?

In the heart's chamber, the Source springs to life,
A symphony of love, cutting through strife.
An eternal melody, soft and clear,
Echoing the cosmos, drawing us near.

Self-love, the key, in this grand co-creation,
A cosmic dance, life's jubilant celebration.
In love, we find strength, in acceptance, our part,
The opening verse of the universe's heart.

From quantum strings to galaxies vast,
We play our notes, in the cosmic cast.
With every heartbeat, every loving notion,
We ripple in rhythm with the universe's ocean.

As we approach the final chapters of our shared journey, let's take a moment to reassert our common purpose. We are not just readers and authors in the traditional sense, but explorers charting the vast expanse of our creative potential.

Our journey has not been one of mere instruction but of shared discovery and mutual inspiration. We're co-creators, equidistant from the universal canvas, painting our destinies with the vibrant colors of our thoughts and actions. And my invitation again, if you feel triggered, please read the book foreword again.

As we delve further, my heartfelt intention is to extend my hand from beside you, inviting you to continue together in this dance of co-creation and exploration. Let's continue to shape our narratives, harnessing the transformative power that lies within us, together.

Chapter 18:

The Higher Self - The Guiding Star in Synchronicities

"We are not human beings having a spiritual experience. We are spiritual beings having a human experience."

- Pierre Teilhard de Chardin

The Higher Self, the Supermind:
The Silent Choreographer

Mysterious patterns often emerge, weaving a tapestry of synchronicities and serendipities. These seemingly unrelated yet profoundly connected events serve as signposts on our journey, guiding our steps and illuminating our path.

As we continue our exploration of the Karmic Multiverse, we encounter a guiding light on our journey - the Higher Self also referred to as the Supermind. This chapter delves into the role of the Higher Self in orchestrating the beautiful dance of synchronicities and serendipities.

The Higher Self, often referred to as the True Self or the Soul, is our deepest, most authentic essence. It transcends our ego-driven identity and connects us with the universal consciousness. The Higher Self is like a silent choreographer, guiding the movements of our universe in the cosmic dance, often through the beautiful patterns of synchronicities and serendipities.

Synchronicities and Serendipities:
The Whisper of the Higher Self

Synchronicities are those moments in life when seemingly unrelated events converge with profound meaning - offering a glimpse into the subtle intelligence that underlies our personal universe. These are not mere coincidences, but precise alignments that speak directly to our inner state, our questions, or our soul's unfolding. They may arrive as a symbol that repeats in different forms, a chance meeting that answers an unspoken prayer, or an external event that perfectly mirrors an internal shift. Often, they appear through numbers - sequences, patterns, or sacred geometries - where mathematics becomes the language of the universe itself, whispering truths beyond words. Synchronicities are the language through which the higher self - or the deeper intelligence within - communicates, offering affirmation, guidance, or redirection.

Serendipities, on the other hand, are unexpected blessings that seem to arise spontaneously, without being consciously sought. They are gentle surprises - pleasant outcomes or helpful encounters that feel orchestrated by a benevolent force, yet come without effort or planning. Where synchronicities often carry a sense of inner dialogue and revelation, serendipities feel like gifts of grace: moments when the universe smiles through beauty, humor, or timing, reminding us that we are supported in ways beyond what we can foresee.

Together, synchronicities and serendipities invite us into a state of receptivity and wonder. One speaks to the depth of our inner alignment; the other to the generosity of life when we live in flow. Both remind us that the multiverse is not random, but relational - that when we walk in trust, the path responds.

The Flow and the Higher Self: A Harmonious Interplay

In the realm of the Higher Self, Flow is not just a state of being but a way of life. It is a harmonious interplay of our inner and outer worlds, a delicate dance that balances our personal desires and the greater good with a deep sense of fulfillment.

When we are attuned to our Higher Self, we naturally find ourselves in a state of flow. We become more receptive to synchronicities and serendipities, recognizing them as the guiding whispers of our Higher Self. These unexpected yet meaningful events become harmonious notes in the melody of our lives, creating a rhythm that resonates with our soul's purpose.

In the cosmic dance of life and mirth,
We encounter our guide, the Higher Self's birth.
Beyond the ego, beyond the known,
In the Karmic Multiverse, its seeds are sown.

Synchronicities, serendipities, patterns so grand,
Are whispers of the Higher Self, a gentle hand.
Guiding our steps, in the cosmic dance,
In the silent rhythm, they enhance.

Listen to the Higher Self, hear its call,
In the dance of the universe, it enthralls.
Through synchronicities, serendipities, the path is shown,
In the Karmic Multiverse, our seeds are sown.

Chapter 19:
Surrender, Trust, and Coincidences: Pathways to Evolution

"The only way to make sense out of change is to plunge into it, move with it, and join the dance."

- Alan Watts

Trust

In our journey of personal and spiritual growth, the concept of trust plays a pivotal role. This trust has two key dimensions: firstly, trusting in our higher self, which represents the wisdom beyond our conscious mind, strongly connected to our subconscious mind, is guiding us through intuition and inner knowing; and secondly, trusting in the universe, a vast and intricate tapestry of life where everything is interconnected in a complex web of synchronicities. To make this more tangible, consider the trust in our higher self as akin to trusting a deeply knowledgeable friend who knows us intimately and guides us with love and wisdom. Trusting the universe, meanwhile, is like floating in a vast ocean, knowing that the currents and tides are part of a grand, harmonious system, leading us to where we need to be. Embracing this trust involves opening our hearts, a process akin to unfolding a flower, petal by petal, revealing the inner core of unconditional love for ourselves and the world. Let's explore this together.

Who holds the steering wheel?

In our exploration of consciousness and the cosmos, we encounter paradoxical truths that challenge our conventional understanding of reality. One such truth, suggested by modern science, is the substantial role our subconscious mind plays in our decision-making process, casting a shadow over the concept of present free will. This revelation, though potentially unsettling, opens up a unique pathway to evolution: surrender, trust in the higher self, the universe, and the recognition of an intricate network of synchronicities.

Research in neuroscience and psychology suggests that our subconscious mind, an unseen driver, steers much of our behavior. Our thoughts, beliefs, and actions often originate from subconscious processes that we're largely unaware of. This understanding challenges the traditional concept of free will, painting it more as an illusion than a reality.

The subconscious mind operates based on tendencies, patterns, and programming rooted in our past experiences, conditioning, and genetic heritage. While this doesn't negate the possibility of conscious choice, it implies that many of our decisions are influenced by factors beyond our immediate conscious control.

The Symphony of Synchronicity: No Coincidences

As we delve into the realm of consciousness and the universe, we find that the mental concept of mere coincidence becomes increasingly untenable. Instead, we find ourselves immersed in a symphony of synchronicities, events interconnected not by cause and effect, but by deep meaning. The universe, it appears, communicates with us through a language of symbols, patterns, and 'coincidences,' orchestrating our path of evolution.

Recognizing these synchronicities requires a shift in perspective: we must transition from linear, cause-and-effect thinking, and embrace a worldview that acknowledges the interconnectedness of all things. In this worldview, nothing is merely coincidental, but rather, each event is a note in the grand symphony of existence.

Surrender: The Gateway to Evolution

In recognizing the limited role of conscious will, we encounter an opportunity for growth and transformation. This opportunity lies in the act of surrender, a conscious choice to let go of our need for control and trust in the higher wisdom of our subconscious mind and the universe.

Surrender is not a sign of weakness or defeat, but rather a powerful act of alignment. It involves letting go of resistance, embracing uncertainty, and allowing the currents of life to guide us. When we surrender, we trust that our subconscious mind, in harmony with the universe, can guide us on a path of evolution, through countless rebirths. This experience of surrender is in tune with our true nature and the cosmos.

Trusting the Higher Self and the Universe

Surrender involves a deep level of trust. This trust is twofold: trust in our higher self, the intuitive wisdom that transcends our conscious mind, and trust in the universe, the grand symphony of existence that we're a part of.

By trusting in our higher self, we open ourselves to insights and guidance that can catalyze profound transformation. Similarly, trusting the universe's complex web of synchronicities allows us to navigate life with a sense of peace and acceptance, facilitating a state of flow that can accelerate our evolution.

Opening the Heart: The Key to Fast Evolution

The key to surrender and trust is opening our hearts, a process that is often challenging and complex. Opening our hearts involves embracing unconditional love for ourselves and the universe, fostering a deep sense of connection and unity. It's not an easy task; It may require grace, intense spiritual practice (sadhana), or the responsible use of entheogenic sacred medicine to facilitate this opening.

When we manage to open our hearts, we align ourselves more closely with the Source, with the rhythm of existence, enabling rapid evolution. The heart becomes a beacon of love and acceptance, radiating its light onto the path of our personal and collective evolution.

While the concept of present free will may be an illusion shaped by our subconscious mind, influenced by our Karma, this understanding can lead us up to a powerful path of evolution. By surrendering control, trusting in our higher self and the universe, acknowledging the symphony of synchronicities, and endeavoring to open our hearts, we can accelerate our journey of growth and transformation, becoming conscious co-creators in the grand symphony of existence.

Reflecting on your own life, how does embracing the concept of surrender and trust alter your response to unexpected changes or coincidences? Can you recall a time when surrendering to the experience led to personal evolution?

In the vast expanse where consciousness resides,
Where the subconscious ebbs and the cosmos collides,
Lies a path of surrender, a journey to the source,
An intricate dance, evolution's course.

In the echo of synchronicity, no coincidence we find,
Each event a symphony, a melody entwined.
In the surrender and trust, in the higher self's embrace,
We find our rhythm in the universe's pace.

Yet the heart's opening, a task both deep and steep,
Requires grace, sadhana, or a leap in the entheogenic leap.
Through love unconditional, a connection we ignite,
A beacon in the darkness, emanating light.

Chapter 20:
Birth, Death, Rebirth: Choosing the Philosophy of Reincarnation?

"Death is not extinguishing the light; it is only putting out the lamp because the dawn has come."

- Rabindranath Tagore

The Cycle of Life, Death, and Rebirth: A Personal Choice

As we navigate the cosmic dance within the Karmic Multiverse, an intriguing concept echoes across various spiritual traditions - the journey of the soul through cycles of birth, death, and rebirth. This process, known as reincarnation, is presented as a vibrant tapestry illustrating each life as a chapter in the soul's grand narrative of evolution. Intriguingly, the adoption of this philosophy is a choice available to each one of us in shaping our personal universe.

The doctrines of Tibetan Buddhism, such as the concept of Bardo, provide a profound description of the interlude between death and subsequent rebirth. This doctrine offers a deep understanding of the odyssey of the soul, not as an imposed reality, but as an optional viewpoint one might choose to incorporate into one's personal universe.

The stages within the Bardo framework serve as influential metaphors for various states of consciousness and significant life transitions. They transcend the limits of post-mortem experiences to offer insights into our living realities, potentially guiding those who choose this philosophy on their path toward liberation and enlightenment.

Likewise, Hindu philosophy presents the law of Karma as a guiding force in this cycle of reincarnation. Each life, under this perspective, offers an opportunity to balance karmic debts and evolve toward Moksha, the liberation from the cycle of birth and death. Our actions and experiences, motivated by desires and attachments, shape our karmic path and influence the course of our soul's journey if we choose to adopt this perspective.

Death as the Greatest Advisor and the Wisdom of Mortality

The awareness of death's inevitability can become a potent catalyst for growth and transformation. It serves as a constant reminder of the fleeting nature of physical existence, inspiring a more profound engagement in the present and a cherishing of each moment as a unique expression of life's vitality.

The consciousness of mortality fosters a deep appreciation of the present, a profound love, authentic actions, passionate pursuit of dreams, and swift forgiveness. The notion of harboring resentment or postponing joy appears futile in the face of the precious and fleeting nature of time - a valuable lesson that can be attributed to death, the silent advisor.

In this context, death becomes a teacher, imparting lessons about detachment, acceptance, and the impermanence of physical existence. It underscores the insight into the futility of clinging to material possessions, status, or even our physical bodies, as these are transient elements of our existence.

Death inspires a focus on the intangible - such as love, wisdom, experiences, and personal growth/evolution - those aspects of our existence that resonate beyond the physical realm and shape the journey of our lives.

The role of death as an advisor also aids in cultivating courage. The understanding that physical existence is temporary can kindle the bravery to step beyond comfort zones, confront fears, and embark on new adventures. If death is viewed as a part of life's journey, the concept of fear undergoes a profound transformation.

The Eternal Dance: A Philosophy to Consider

Life, in its most fundamental essence, is a continuous cycle of creation and destruction, birth and death, beginnings and endings. This cycle, ceaselessly turning, is a universal law reflected in every facet of existence, from natural phenomena to the depths of our individual lives. It is not a linear progression but an eternal dance, an ebb and flow pervading the cosmos.

Each ending, under the lens of reincarnation, is not a finality, but a doorway to a new beginning, a new form, a new expression of existence. This perspective of death and destruction as necessary processes enabling rebirth and creation is available to anyone who chooses to incorporate it into their worldview.

Amidst the tumultuous dance of creation and destruction, adopting the philosophy of reincarnation offers a profound sense of tranquility. This peace arises from recognizing the larger pattern, and understanding that destruction is not an end but a transformation. This suggests the dance of existence is not random chaos but an intricate choreography, a harmonious interplay of forces facilitating the evolution of the cosmos, for those who choose to see it this way.

Collective Karma and the Shadow Dance in Our Personal Universe

Having the eternal in our focus, we are invited to embrace a more positive perspective on the seemingly darker aspects of existence, like mass tragedies and catastrophes. These events, while heart-wrenching in their immediate impact, offer a different hue to the majestic picture of the personal journey of the soul.

In the grand continuum of the soul's evolution, as proposed by the reincarnation philosophy, each life and death is but a fleeting moment. The soul's journey, spanning countless lifetimes, suggests that the pain experienced in one life is a brief instance in the eternal cycle of reincarnation. From this perspective, the human beings lost in mass tragedies may be seen as transitioning into another phase of the endless journey of their souls, potentially reborn countless times as the sand grains in a desert, each experience shaping their evolving consciousness.

These events are indeed tragic. We can only glean a glimpse of "understanding" by seeing them in the larger spectrum of experiences that a soul undergoes in its quest for evolution and understanding. While we mourn the losses, we also acknowledge them as integral parts of the soul's journey, contributing in ways beyond our understanding to the richness and diversity of the soul's experiences.

This positive outlook toward life and death, rooted in the philosophy of reincarnation, may help to transform our understanding of tragedies. Instead of viewing them as mere endpoints, we begin to see them as transitions, moments of transformation that lead to new beginnings. Every ending is a prelude to a rebirth, a continuation of the soul's adventure across the cosmic tapestry.

Additionally, it is important to remember the concept of back-fill people introduced earlier in our discussions on simulation theory. These entities, which do not possess an independent consciousness but are reflections of our own, play a unique role in the cosmic narrative. In the context of mass tragedies and catastrophes, many of the Humans involved are these back-fill beings, serving as mirrors to our consciousness in our personal universe. Their presence and participation in these events are not expressions of individual soul journeys, but rather, they are manifestations of our karmic energies. This understanding adds another layer to our perception of these events, viewing them not just as random occurrences but as deeply intertwined with the collective psyche and its manifestation in our shared reality.

This perspective allows us to view life's challenges, including mass tragedies, with a sense of deep understanding and acceptance. It encourages us to appreciate the full spectrum of experiences as essential to the soul's growth and evolution. In this light, every event, joyous or sorrowful, becomes a valuable chapter in the soul's eternal story.

Embracing the Cosmic Self: Highlights of the Soul's Journey

One of the highlights of the soul's journey across countless lifetimes and countless experiences is the embrace of the cosmic self. This is the realization of our inherent interconnectedness with all existence and the understanding that our individual consciousness is a part of the universal consciousness.

In the Upanishads, one of the oldest Hindu scriptures, the spiritual journey of the soul is beautifully articulated through two profound phrases. "Aham Brahmasmi," meaning "I am Brahman." 'Aham' refers to the self that is constant and ever-present, and 'Brahman' is the entirety, the whole that is ever-full. This profound statement from the Brihadaranyaka Upanishad expresses the realization that the self is not separate but is the universal whole.

The second phrase, "Tat Tvam Asi," which translates to "You are that," signifies that the individual self (Atman) and the universal essence (Brahman) are one and the same. It marks the final absolute self-recognition, the ultimate understanding and acknowledgment that the individual self (Atman) and the universal self (Brahman) are one and the same. Have you heard of the greeting "Namaste" before, and do you know its meaning? How do you resonate with its meaning?

In the dance of the cosmic multiverse, bold and grand,
Echoes the cycle of life, an eternal band.
Birth, death, and rebirth, a soul's vibrant song,
A choice of belief, where we can belong.

The Tibetan Bardo, a profound guide,
In the interlude of lives, it resides.
Hindu Karma, a force so wise,
In the cycle of reincarnation, our soul's prize.

Death, the advisor, silent and true,
Teaches of fleeting time, in every hue.
Inspires love, courage, and passionate dreams,
In the face of mortality, life gleams.

Chapter 21:
The Cosmic Illusion - The Higher Self's Enigmatic Dance

"Reality is merely an illusion, albeit a very persistent one."

- Albert Einstein

The Cosmic Lie: The Grand Choreography of the Higher Self

With all of this knowledge, we encounter an enigmatic truth: the grand Maya-Illusion orchestrated by the Higher Self / the Universe. This chapter explores this cosmic illusion, the narratives of prophets and gods, and the profound implications for our journey.

Our deepest essence is part of the universal consciousness that governs our personal universe. Curiously, that Higher Self, or the Universe itself, maintains a grand illusion, a lie, masking the ultimate truth of our existence. This cosmic illusion, also known as Maya in Hindu philosophy, is akin to a veiling dance, obscuring the ultimate reality.

Prophets, Gods, and the Game of Illusion

Throughout history, prophets and gods have played significant roles in our collective understanding of the universe. They shape our beliefs, guide our actions, and thoroughly influence our lives. These divine and enlightened beings have been viewed as beacons of truth, guiding humanity through its spiritual and moral evolution. Yet, here lies a subtle nuance: while they offer profound insights, spiritual revelations, and moral directives, they too are manifestations within the grand illusion. Their stories, teachings, and actions not only deepen the mystery, making our journey of discovery richer and more layered but also serve as components of the cosmic illusion, ensuring a long, if not endless, journey.

The Purpose of the Lie: A Dance of Discovery

The illusion or Maya, despite its veil, serves a profound purpose. It promotes exploration, growth, and evolution, transforming our life into a journey of discovery and self-realization. The illusion, however painful, ensures that our lifetime within the Karmic Multiverse is not a short performance but a continuous liberating process of healing, learning, spiritual evolution, and unification.

The Universe as a Conscious Creator: The Healing Dance

Integral to the enlightening truth is the concept of the universe as a conscious creator, a divine entity that both orchestrates the cosmic illusion but also supports our healing and growth. This perspective shifts our understanding of the universe from a passive backdrop to being an active participant in our journey, guiding us, nurturing us, and facilitating our transformation.

The conscious universe communicates with us through synchronicities, serendipities, intuitive insights, and deep profound experiences that touch the core of our being. It supports us in navigating the dance of illusion, providing us with the tools and opportunities to unveil the truth and to heal.

Healing, in the context of this book, is not just about physical recovery. It encompasses emotional, psychological, trauma, ancestral, and spiritual healing and beyond. It's about restoring our alignment with the universal rhythm, harmonizing our dance with the cosmic melody, and releasing the discordant notes that cause suffering and dissonance.

In the conscious universe, healing is a dance of transformation. It involves shedding old patterns, beliefs, and identities that no longer serve us and embracing new ways of being that reflect our deepest truth. It's about becoming attuned to the cosmic rhythm, aligning our intentions, actions, thoughts, and emotions with the flow of the universe.

The Truths Dance in the Karmic Multiverse

Truth, much like the concept of karma, is not a static entity. It is a dynamic interplay of perspectives, experiences, and realities. It is as vast and diverse as the multiverse itself and as singular and unique as each individual consciousness navigating through the cosmic dance. As such, embracing the dance of truth requires an open heart and mind, a willingness to question, and the courage to seek.

The dance of truth is, therefore, not merely a quest for knowledge, but a journey of transformation. It is about transcending the limitations of the ego and realizing one's true nature as a divine being. It is about recognizing the interconnectedness of all things, the cosmic harmony that underlies the universe, and the unconditional love that is the ultimate truth of existence. If you now feel lost as to what is true and what is not, you are invited to revisit the chapter on decentralized governance.

In the grand ballet of the cosmic sphere,
A dance of illusion appears so clear.
The Higher Self, the Universe wide,
In the dance of Maya, they preside.

Prophets and gods, narratives unfold,
In the cosmic illusion, stories are told.
Guiding our dance, in rhythm and rhyme,
In the Karmic Multiverse, they chime.

The illusion, a veil, yet a guide in disguise,
A dance of discovery, before our eyes.
Through prophets, gods, the truth we glean,
In the cosmic dance, the unseen seen.

Chapter 22

The Power of Intentions

"What we think, we become"

- Siddhartha Buddha

The Quantum Mechanics of Intentions

In the grand fabric of the multiverse, where quantum oscillations dance to the rhythm of consciousness, our intentions play a pivotal role. Intentions, which can be defined as purposeful mental drives that guide our actions, are not merely abstract thoughts. They are powerful energetic expressions that can shape our personal universe and potentially influence the greater multiverse.

When we set an intention, we are consciously choosing a specific outcome or state of being. This act of conscious choice is much like an observer measuring a quantum system, thereby influencing the system's state. Our intentions, therefore, act as energetic signals sent out into the quantum field, influencing the very fabric of our reality.

Intentions and the Karmic Multiverse

In the context of the Karmic Multiverse, our intentions serve as the seeds we sow into the cosmic soil. They are the vibrational frequencies we emit, resonating with the frequencies of the multiverse. When our intentions are positive, we align ourselves with positive outcomes, creating a resonance that can attract favorable circumstances in our lives.

This is not to say that intentions alone can manifest a desired reality. We must couple them with action, guided by wisdom and responsibility.

Yet, the power of our intentions sets the course, serving as a compass pointing toward our desired reality.

Mastering the Influence of Intentions:

Harnessing the power of intentions requires mindfulness, clarity, and emotional alignment. Mindfulness allows us to realize our underlying intentions. Clarity helps us define our intentions, aligning them with our highest values and goals. Emotional alignment ensures that our feelings resonate with our intentions, amplifying their power.

When your intentions are clear, aligned, and powered by positive emotions, they become potent forces shaping your infinite universe; they influence your thoughts, emotions, and actions and you become the alchemist for your desired reality. When our clear intentions are like seeds sown into the cosmic soil, how do you cultivate the quality of your intentions to ensure they yield the most beneficial outcomes for yourself and those around you? What practices or mindsets might you adopt to align your intentions with the greater good within the infinite multiverse?

In the realm of the shaman, where spirit meets skin,
The power of intention is where it begins.
An echo in the silence, a whisper in the wind,
A call to the cosmos, where endings and beginnings blend.

Intentions are cast like seeds in the night,
In the fertile soil of the soul, kissed by starlight.
With a shaman's wisdom, intentions take flight,
Through the veil of the mundane, into the night.

They ripple through the quantum, they sing in the void,
In the dance of the cosmos, they're perfectly poised.
They resonate with the multiverse, in a rhythm so grand,
In the cosmic ballet, they make their stand.

Chapter 23:
The Infinite Dance
in the Cosmic Theater

"There was no 'before' the beginning of our universe, because once upon a time there was no time."

- John D. Barrow

Understanding Infinity: A Cosmic Paradox

As we embark on this chapter, we find ourselves standing at the edge of an unfathomable abyss, gazing into the depths of infinity. Infinity, an enigma wrapped in the fabric of existence, is a concept that both astounds and humbles us. It is an idea that stretches the limits of our understanding, challenging the constraints of our finite minds.

Infinity is a paradox that lies at the heart of the multiverse. We live in a universe that is finite yet unbounded, limited in its physical extent yet infinite in its potential. This understanding of infinity is not a contradiction, but a testament to the multidimensional nature of reality.

The concept of infinity tells us that there is no end to the universe, no boundary where existence stops and nothingness begins. Instead, the universe curves in on itself, creating a loop of cosmic dance that never ends. This loop is not a limitation, but an expression of infinite potential, beautifully visualized by the Yin and Yang symbol.

And within this looping dance lies a deeper truth: time itself is not linear, but vertical. In Vertical Time, all versions of you - past lives, future incarnations, and alternate selves - exist now, layered like harmonics in a grand cosmic chord. When you shift your consciousness in the present, that shift ripples not just forward, but backward and sideways across these layers, rewriting your participation in infinity.

Infinity in the Quantum-Karmic Model

The quantum-karmic model of the universe provides an exciting lens through which to explore the concept of infinity. Quantum mechanics teaches us about the infinite potentialities that exist in the quantum field, where particles exist in a state of superposition until observed. This superposition is a dance of infinite possibilities, a dance that collapses into a singular reality through the act of conscious observation.

Karma, or action, shapes the probabilities in the quantum field, guiding the dance of potentialities. Yet, the infinite possibilities remain, echoing the boundless nature of the multiverse. Our choices, intentions, expressions of free will, create the karma that acts as the observer, determining the wave function of infinite possibilities into a chosen reality.

But the implications stretch further. When a belief takes root deep enough - when it becomes not just an idea, but a foundational truth anchored deep in your Karma - you begin to influence not only the path ahead, but the origin of your personal universe. Your belief becomes the key that opens the door not just to a new future, but to a rewritten past. If you believe your soul emerged from the Garden of Eden, then your universe begins to weave that myth into the roots of its fabric. If you see yourself as a star-born traveler, that becomes your genesis. The multiverse, in its infinite generosity, will begin to arrange evidence, people, synchronicities - even scientific discoveries - that confirm the story you've chosen.

The Infinite Dance of Consciousness

If we consider consciousness as the fundamental reality, as proposed by some interpretations of quantum mechanics, then we are participants in an infinite dance. Each conscious act, every thought, emotion, and action, is a step in this dance, a ripple in the infinite ocean of consciousness.

Our personal universe is a unique expression of this infinite consciousness, a single thread in the cosmic tapestry of existence. We are both the dancers and the choreographers in this infinite dance, shaping and being shaped by the cosmic rhythms of the multiverse.

Embracing Infinity: A Path to Spiritual Evolution

Embracing infinity is not about comprehending the incomprehensible, but about surrendering to the mysteries of existence. It's about recognizing our place in the cosmic theater and acknowledging our role in the infinite dance of consciousness.

As we surrender to the rhythm of this dance, we align ourselves with the flow of the universe, guiding our spiritual evolution. We understand that our individual journey, though seemingly finite, is an essential part of the infinite dance of existence.

This realization empowers us to shape our dance within the personal universe with intentionality. It invites us to live fully, explore fearlessly, and above all, to believe courageously. For belief is not merely a lens - it is the sculptor of timelines, the author of beginnings, the magnet of worlds. Whatever you believe deeply enough - cosmologically, spiritually, even scientifically - will eventually echo back to you as truth. Not because you imposed it on reality, but because you tuned yourself into the infinite stream where that version of reality already exists.

In the grand theater of existence, we stand,
Gazing into infinity, a concept so grand.
An infinite dance on the cosmic stage,
Unfolds in the book of the multiverse, page by page.

Quantum fields whisper tales of the arcane,
Of infinite potentials in a cosmic domain.
In the dance of particles, reality unfurls,
Weaving a cosmic tapestry, in quantum swirls.

Consciousness, the dancer, in this infinite ballet,
Shapes and is shaped by the cosmic array.
In the rhythm of existence, we find our role,
As dancers and choreographers, we embrace the whole.

Chapter 24:
Regeneration and Healing: The Spiritual Ripple of Wellness

"Healing yourself is connected with healing others."

- Yoko Ono

Healing Yourself:
The First Step to Universal Healing

In the cosmic dance of life, regeneration, and healing form an integral part of the rhythm. Just as galaxies are born and die only to be reborn again in the cosmic ballet, so too are we, as conscious beings, given the opportunity to heal, grow, and renew ourselves. A timeless shamanic saying holds a profound truth: "If you want to heal the world, first you need to heal yourself, then your family, then your community. After that, the whole world will heal on its own."

The first step towards world healing begins with healing ourselves. As conscious beings, we are vessels of energy, vibrating at unique frequencies that shape our personal universe. Our thoughts, intentions, emotions, and actions leave energetic imprints in this personal universe, creating patterns that define our karmic evolution.

When we are in harmony, our personal universe resonates with the multiverse, creating a beautiful dance in the cosmic ballet. However, blockages, imbalances, or unresolved issues can disrupt this harmony, causing dissonance in our dance.

Healing ourselves involves recognizing these dissonances and actively working to resolve them. This requires deep introspection, acceptance, and transformative action. Practices such as meditation, yoga, mindfulness, or resorting to psychotherapy can help in identifying and healing these blockages. Interestingly, many find that a single session with a shaman working with entheogens can have an impact equivalent to ten years of psychotherapy. This powerful sacred medicine used responsibly and under expert guidance, can facilitate profound root healing, and spiritual and emotional insights, accelerating the journey toward inner harmony. By healing ourselves through these varied means, we restore balance in our personal universe, enabling us to dance in sync with the greater cosmic rhythm.

Dissolving Karma and Healing Through the Dance of Receptive Grace

In this sacred life, we often find ourselves cradled in the arms of circumstances that are laden with pain, draped in the veils of challenge, and seemingly woven from the threads of hardship. Yet, within these very moments, there lies a hidden gateway, an invitation to a dance that transcends time, a dance that dissolves the spirals of Karma that have twirled through the ages.

Envision, if you will, the graceful dance of a leaf, descending from the lofty heights of its arboreal home. It does not resist the wind's embrace; it does not struggle against the inevitable descent. Instead, it surrenders to the whims of the breeze, twirling and swirling in a dance of acceptance. In this surrender, in this act of receiving the wind's caress, there lies profound tranquility, a silent acknowledgment that every descent is part of a greater ascent, every fall a prelude to a rise.

This is the sacred dance we are beckoned to when life presents us with its tapestry of pain and challenge. We are called not to resist, not to fight, but to receive. To receive each experience with the

tender embrace of the feminine energy that cradles the universe, the energy that nurtures, that accepts, that loves unconditionally.

In this act of receiving, of allowing ourselves to be caressed by the winds of experience, there is no quest for wisdom, no search for teaching. For Karma, in its infinite wisdom, does not seek to teach; it seeks to resolve. It seeks to untangle the knots that we have woven through our actions and reactions, through our resistance and our fears.

By staying in this feminine energy of receiving, we become like the leaf in the wind, dancing to the rhythm of the universe. We allow Karma to work itself out, to dissolve its patterns, to free us from the cycles that have bound us. In this dance of receiving, there is no struggle, no strife; there is only the gentle unfolding of being, the soft whisper of liberation that echoes through the corridors of time.

Healing the Family: The Resonance of Healing

When we heal ourselves, the effects resonate beyond our personal boundaries to influence those closest to us - our family. Our personal universe is closely linked with the personal universes of our family members, creating a shared family universe.

The healing changes we make in ourselves can create a ripple effect, influencing the family universe's energetic patterns. This influence can catalyze healing transformations in our family members, encouraging them to seek their healing and growth.

However, it's important to understand that each person's healing journey is unique and must be self-initiated. As such, our role in our family's healing is to provide a supportive and nurturing environment that fosters growth and transformation.

Healing the Community: Expanding the Ripple of Wellness

As our healing journey progresses, its effects ripple further outwards to influence our broader communities. Our communities are intricate webs of interconnected personal universes, each contributing to the collective energy.

When we heal ourselves, our elevated vibrations will influence and inspire healing transformations within our community. We become beacons of healing, encouraging others to embark on their healing journeys. This process can manifest in various ways, such as promoting wellness practices, advocating for mental health, or creating safe spaces for sharing and support.

The Global Healing: The Shamanic Vision

The shamanic saying concludes with a profound promise: after healing ourselves, our families, and our communities, the whole world will heal on its own. This is based on the understanding of the interconnectedness of all existence.

Our world is a cosmic dance floor where each conscious being contributes to the grand choreography. When we initiate healing at an individual level, the ripples of transformation eventually reach the farthest corners of our shared existence, influencing the global consciousness. This cascading effect of healing fosters a global environment of wellness, harmony, and unity - precisely the conditions needed for the world to heal itself.

Healing is a deeply personal yet profoundly universal journey. It starts within us and ripples outwards, influencing our families, communities, and eventually, the world. By embracing our role in this healing process, we contribute to the grand dance of the Karmic Multiverse, facilitating a cosmic symphony of wellness, harmony, and regeneration.

In the dance of life where stars are born and die,
A whisper of healing starts with an inner sigh.
Self-love, acceptance, the first steps we tread,
In the mirror of self, the world is gently led.

Beyond the hearth, the ripple extends,
To the community's edge, where the self transcends.
A beacon of healing, softly we glow,
In the tapestry of life, love's seeds we sow.

Across the cosmic stage, the ripple flows,
In the heart of the world, a healing rose.
The Shaman's promise, the world reborn anew,
In each healing heart, the universe finds its hue.

Chapter 25:
The Interconnected Dance: Regeneration, Justice, and Global Harmony

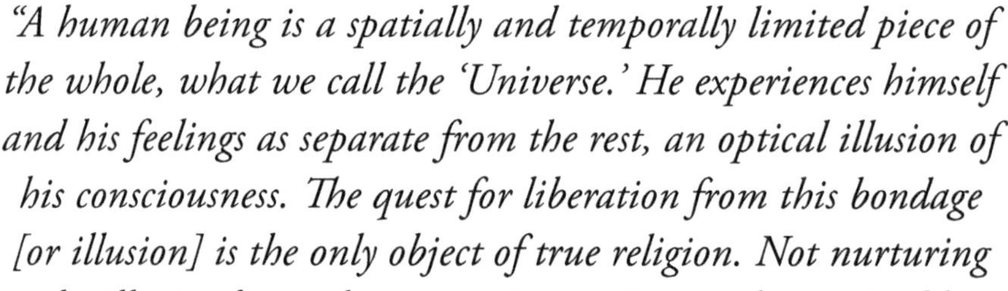

"A human being is a spatially and temporally limited piece of the whole, what we call the 'Universe.' He experiences himself and his feelings as separate from the rest, an optical illusion of his consciousness. The quest for liberation from this bondage [or illusion] is the only object of true religion. Not nurturing the illusion but only overcoming it gives us the attainable measure of inner peace"

- Albert Einstein

Social Coherence: Born from Interconnectedness

As we continue our exploration of the Karmic Multiverse, we remember the illuminating truth - the profound interconnectedness of all existence. This principle of interconnectedness has wide-ranging implications that stretch beyond the metaphysical sphere. It actively influences social coherence, environmental regeneration, and our responsive approach to global opportunities.

In the cosmic symphony, every participant contributes to the grand composition. Recognizing our interconnectedness, we begin to appreciate that each player's experience resonates throughout the cosmic arena. This understanding casts a transformative light on social coherence.

When we acknowledge our interconnectedness, we naturally cultivate empathy and compassion, fostering a culture of mutual respect and understanding. We begin to appreciate the diversity of experiences and perspectives that enrich our shared cosmic symphony. Moreover, we can utilize our unique roles to champion equality and fairness, creating harmonious reverberations throughout the multiverse.

Environmental Regeneration:
The Symphony of Renewal

Our interconnectedness profoundly extends to the rhythms of nature, binding us deeply to Earth's cycles of renewal. We are not passive observers but active co-creators within nature's living tapestry. This vibrant kinship calls us to listen carefully and harmonize with the melodies of environmental regeneration.

By attuning our lives to nature's patterns, nurturing ecosystems, and actively participating in their restoration, we amplify the song of Earth's revival. In aligning our actions with nature's wisdom, we become integral notes within the great cosmic symphony, harmoniously resonating with the flourishing rhythms of the living Earth and the expansive dance of the multiverse.

Global Opportunities:
Resonant Symphony of Collective Consciousness

Our interconnectedness offers a fresh perspective on global opportunities, and in this light, the Global Consciousness Project (GCP) stands as a pivotal revelation, shedding light on the profound interconnectedness between human consciousness and the physical realm. Originating from Princeton University, the GCP harnesses a network of random number generators (RNGs) globally, seeking correlations between significant global events and anomalies in data patterns. This groundbreaking project proposes that moments of widespread human emotion - be they joy, grief, or anticipation - may subtly influence these RNGs, unveiling a previously hidden layer of interconnectedness.

This realization beckons a radical redefinition of consciousness and its interplay with the physical world. Accepting the GCP's findings compels us to reconsider the nature of consciousness as potentially integral to the fundamental workings of the universe, particularly in the realm of quantum mechanics. Such an understanding could transform our perception of reality, positioning consciousness as a pivotal factor in the universe's fabric.

Our global opportunities are thus seen in a new light. Health advancements, peaceful collaborations, and economic growth are not merely isolated developments; they are interwoven patterns within our cosmic symphony. This perspective, inspired by the GCP, challenges us to envision a world where collective thoughts and emotions significantly shape our reality.

Embracing this interconnected dance, as illuminated by the GCP, we approach global challenges with a renewed, holistic mindset. We are not just participants in the world's unfolding story but active creators within a vast, dynamic symphony of collective consciousness. Our solutions must, therefore, harmonize with this broader cosmic symphony, aiming for prosperity and balance at every level.

Regenerative Governance: Distributed Power and Shamanic Consensus Circles

Regenerative governance embodies the dance between order and chaos, mirroring the cosmic balance of Yin and Yang. This model harmonizes masculine efficiency and feminine nurturance, advocating for self-governance through collective wisdom. It embraces concepts like Heterarchy for structured decision-making, complemented by shamanic consensus circles that nurture deep community connections. This approach fosters a dynamic equilibrium, allowing organizations and communities to thrive in harmony with nature's rhythms, acting like ecosystems and embodying the essence of regenerative living.

Shamanic Consensus Talking-Circle Process (No Facilitator Needed):

1. **Opening the Circle:** The circle begins with a collective moment of silence, prayer, or a spiritual practice like chanting "AUM." This ritual facilitates connection and oneness and sets a respectful and mindful atmosphere. The spirit of Mother Earth is invited, along with other spiritual beings who are supportive of the group.

2. **Use of the Talking Stick:** A talking stick is passed clockwise (Sunwise) around the circle, signifying each participant's opportunity to speak.

3. **Proposal Presentation as a 'Seed':** When an individual has a proposal, they call for consensus while holding the talking stick. By presenting it, the proposal is metaphorically shaped like a 'seed' of masculine energy, ready to be planted in the feminine 'womb' of the group's collective silence.

4. **Absolute Silence for Consensus:** The key to reaching consensus is absolute silence as the talking stick is passed around the circle back to the proposer. If the stick completes a full circle without any sound - no words, affirmations like "Aho," "Amen," or "Yes," or any other noises - the proposal is considered accepted. This silence represents the unanimous agreement of the group, spirit, and divine mother.

5. **Option for Questions:** If a participant needs clarification, they can place down the talking stick to ask a question to the group. Other participants may raise their hands to answer, creating a brief Q&A exchange. Alternatively, the participant can direct a question to a specific person, at which point the talking stick is passed directly to that individual for their response, and then

returned to the original asker. After the question is addressed, the normal circle process resumes.

6. **Closing the Circle:** The circle is closed by a call for consensus to end the meeting. This is again determined by the silent passage of the talking stick around the entire circle. If anyone in the group wishes to leave before the official closing, they are free to do so, but the group as a whole remains until a consensus for closure is silently reached.

Heartsharing Talking-Circle Process (No Facilitator Needed):

1. **Opening the Circle:** Start with a group activity like a moment of silence, a short meditation, or a group chant to create a unified and respectful atmosphere.

2. **Guidelines Agreement:** As a group, we agree on the guidelines, emphasizing the importance of speaking from the heart, listening without judgment, and confidentiality. We express our own experiences and perspectives, without directly addressing anyone and we respect time limits for sharing.

3. **Heart Sharing:** Participants take turns holding the talking object to share their feelings and thoughts. Others in the circle listen attentively and empathetically, without interruptions.

4. **Passing the Talking Object:** After sharing, the speaker passes the object to the next person anticlockwise (Earthwise), who may choose to speak, sit in silence, or pass it along.

5. **Consensual Closing:** The circle is closed by a call for consensus to end the meeting. If it completes a full circle without anyone

making a noise, the meeting is considered closed by silent consensus. Participants can leave before the official closing, but the group remains until this consensus is reached.

Regenerative Finance: Catalyst for Regenerative Growth

In the realm of finance, our focus must transition from mere sustainability to proactive regenerative economies. This shift acknowledges a critical juncture in our collective journey - we are at a point where sustaining is insufficient; we must engage in active regeneration to heal and rejuvenate our world. This transformative approach entails channeling financial resources into initiatives that not only revitalize ecosystems and foster social equity but also bolster holistic well-being. It's about strategic investment in projects that yield more than financial returns; these endeavors contribute significantly to the health and vitality of the planet and all its inhabitants.

Integral to this vision is the adoption of circular economy models, particularly within bioregions and communities. Such models are instrumental in encouraging local, grassroots regenerative practices, bringing the abundance of Mother Nature back to the grassroots level. By embracing these circular systems, we support a sustainable cycle of resource use and recovery, ensuring that local communities thrive in harmony with their natural environments. This holistic approach to finance and resource management is pivotal in creating a world where every investment and economic action nourishes and enriches the Earth, paving the way for a future that is not only sustainable but abundantly regenerative.

Regenerative Agriculture:
The Cornerstone of Healing Our Biosphere

Regenerative agriculture stands as a cornerstone in healing our biosphere. This practice goes beyond sustainable farming, actively improving soil health, increasing biodiversity, and restoring natural ecosystems. It encompasses permaculture, agroforestry, and organic farming, methods that work in harmony with nature rather than against it. These practices sequester carbon, enhance water retention, and support a diverse range of life forms, demonstrating a profound respect for the Earth and its intricate web of life.

A Symphony of Unity, Prosperity,
and Regeneration

Our cosmic symphony is a testament to the interconnectedness of all existence. Every note we play, every rhythm we create, resonates throughout the multiverse. By embracing this interconnectedness, we can navigate together our dance with wisdom and compassion. We advocate for regenerative governance and finance, social coherence, champion environmental regeneration, and collaboratively respond to global opportunities, all while contributing to a harmonious cosmic orchestra. What role do you see for yourself in contributing to the grand symphony of global harmony? Can you identify actions or changes in perspective that might align your personal journey with the collective pursuit of regeneration and justice?

In the grand waltz of the cosmos, a truth sublime,
Interconnection weaves its rhythm, in space and time.
In the dance of existence, each twirl, each bend,
Echoes in the multiverse, from start to end.

From social coherence to nature's sweet song,
Our dance shapes the universe, vibrant and strong.
In every step, in every beat, in every elation,
We co-create a world of unity and regeneration.

Global opportunities, like stars in the night,
In our cosmic dance, they sparkle bright.
Together we dance, creating ripples of light,
Guiding the multiverse to a future bright.

Chapter 26:
Mastering Our Destiny

"The only person you are destined to become is the person you decide to be."

- Ralph Waldo Emerson

Becoming the Designers of Our Personal Universe

We all possess the innate ability to shape our personal reality - a concept echoed in both ancient spiritual wisdom and modern quantum physics. Through our intentions, thoughts, emotions, and actions, we create vibrational patterns that resonate with the energies of the multiverse, attracting experiences and circumstances that align with these vibrations.

By becoming conscious co-creators, we can harness this power to manifest our desires, align with our highest good, and contribute positively to the grand dance of the multiverse. This involves cultivating mindfulness, maintaining positive thought patterns, and taking intentional actions aligned with our highest values and goals.

Cultivating the Eternal: An Invitation to Spiritual Labor

The material dimension, with all its splendor and spectacle, is but a playful shadow cast by the luminous spirit. It is the grand Lila, the divine play, where we dress and act, not realizing that the roles we embody are fleeting characters in a cosmic script. One should not refrain from concrete action in the physical realm; rather, let us redirect our energies to where they matter most.

To work in the spiritual world is not to abandon action but to elevate it. It is to act with an awakened heart, in the spirit of Integral Yoga and with the knowledge that each deed is a seed that when sown with conscious intent, blossoms into realities beyond the confines of time and space. In this sacred garden, our thoughts, emotions, and actions are the tools with which we cultivate a destiny that resonates with the pulse of the universe.

You are invited to consider a different kind of labor - a labor of the soul. Let us become farmers for the action of Spirit, for it is in the spiritual world that the seeds of our actions find eternal soil. Here, in the realm of the intangible, is where the true work unfolds.

In the cosmic dance, we find our way,
Mastering our destiny, in the cosmic fray.
With each thought, each beat of the heart,
In the multiverse, our dance takes part.

Conscious creation, the artist's brush,
In the cosmic canvas, a serene hush.
With every step, every beat, every notion,
We shape the multiverse, with our emotion.

In the grand dance, a harmony is born,
In the cosmic rhythm, our path is worn.
The dance continues, the music plays,
In the cosmic dance, we find our ways.

Conclusion
Synergies of Wisdom - The Dance Continues

"The privilege of a lifetime is to become who you truly are."

- Carl Jung

Exploring the rhythms and learning the movements of the Multiverse, we come to understand that this cosmic dance is an ongoing process - a dance that continues to evolve, transform, and unfold with each passing moment.

Quantum mechanics and Eastern philosophies, seemingly disparate, share a profound resonance in the cosmic dance. Both suggest a universe intimately responsive to our consciousness, a reality woven by our intentions and observations. This synergy opens up new dimensions of understanding, bridging the gap between science and spirituality, and enhancing our dance within the Karmic Multiverse.

Kindling the Inner Light:
A Journey Toward Liberation

As you turn the last page of this book and re-enter your daily life, remember the flame that has been kindled in your heart. This flame symbolizes the wisdom and understanding you've gained, a beacon of resilience and unconditional love. It's a source of healing, transformation, and unlimited free energy, not just for you, but for your entire personal universe.

Every experience, whether joyful or challenging, serves to strengthen and nourish this flame. The doubts and negativity from others won't extinguish it; they'll only make it burn more fiercely. And in times of sadness or difficulty, this flame won't be smothered; instead, these moments will give it even more fuel to grow.

This flame represents our capacity for unconditional love, a force that multiplies with every act of kindness and compassion we extend to others. It's a reminder that giving love doesn't deplete our reserves; it enhances them.

Keep this flame burning brightly within you. Let it be a source of continuous healing, personal transformation, and a wellspring of energy for all aspects of your life and the beings around you. It's a beacon that guides you, illuminating your path with purpose, understanding, and ever-deepening compassion.

Quantum Sovereignty: The Ongoing Journey of Cosmic Resonance

Let us remember: each philosophy, each theory, and each tradition is an integral part of the cosmic dance - a dance that celebrates diversity, cherishes unity, and echoes the infinite wisdom of the cosmos.

Now that you have journeyed through the spiraling galaxies of thought within these pages, you stand at the cusp of a majestic realm. This knowledge you hold is not merely information; it is the chisel in your hands, ready to sculpt the ether of your personal universe. The sacred power that pulses at the core of this wisdom is yours to claim.

Own it, let it course through you, as vital and potent as the life force itself. Let it empower you to carve out a reality that resonates with the deepest vibrations of your being. In your hands, this knowledge can become the scepter with which you command the elements of the quantum realm, bending the very fabric of existence to your will, your vision, and your purpose.

Should you choose, let this be the crucible from which you may forge a philosophy uniquely your own. Let each word, each concept, and each quantum entanglement you've encountered in these pages be the ingredients for your alchemical transformation. You are free to blend, to bend, to juxtapose against the philosophies that have walked with humanity through the ages.

Your personal universe awaits your design, a cosmos crafted not by fate nor by the random hand of chance, but by the deliberate, conscious strokes of your own intent. The multiverse is your canvas, your playground, your laboratory. Every thought, every intention, every dream is a brush stroke on this grand mural.

Take this knowledge, this sacred power, with the reverence and the revolutionary spirit it deserves. Go forth and create, not in the image of this or any philosophy that has come before, but in the image of your most authentic self. This is your birthright, your adventure, your quantum leap into the infinite.

As we close the dance, a new one begins,
In the cosmic rhythm, the soul spins.
The journey continues, beyond time and space,
In the cosmic dance, we find our grace.

In the dance of the multiverse, we find our song,
To the cosmic rhythm, we belong.
With every step, every beat, every notion,
We shape the multiverse, with our devotion.

The dance continues, the music plays on,
In the cosmic dance, we have just begun.
With love and gratitude, we find our way,
In the cosmic dance, we sway.

Practical Steps to Implement

Meditation: In embracing the practice of meditation, focus on nurturing equanimity toward your thoughts. This approach involves observing your mental processes impartially, without getting entangled in their content. Such balanced observation gradually transforms your mind from a relentless transmitter of thoughts and actions into a receptive space. In this cultivated stillness, you become open to the universe's subtle communications, allowing you to receive intuitive insights and answers to deeper queries. It's in this serene quietude that the universe's wisdom gently permeates your consciousness, offering guidance and clarity previously obscured by the continuous hum of mental activity.

Affirmations: Use positive affirmations to reshape your thought patterns. Affirmations are positive statements that can help you overcome self-sabotaging thoughts. They can be based on personal goals or qualities you wish to develop.

Conscious Consumption: Be mindful of what you consume, both physically and mentally. This includes the food you eat, the media you consume, and the company you keep. Try to make choices that are beneficial to your well-being and aligned with your spiritual growth.

Fasting: Incorporate periods of fasting into your routine. This can be done in various ways, such as intermittent fasting, where you restrict your eating to a specific window of time each day, or more prolonged fasting periods. Fasting provides numerous benefits, including cleansing and detoxifying the body, enhancing mental clarity and discipline, and promoting spiritual growth.

Setting Intentions: Identify your desires and goals. Visualize your intention as already achieved, feeling its emotional impact. This emotional alignment amplifies its quantum resonance. Finally, couple your intention with decisive action, grounding its energy into the physical world.

Nature Connection: Spend time in nature regularly. This can be as simple as going for a walk in a park or relaxing beside a lake, river, or stream. Connecting with nature can provide a sense of peace and perspective, and can help you feel more grounded and attuned to the natural rhythms of the universe.

Journaling: Maintain a regular journaling practice. This can serve as a tool for self-reflection, allowing you to track your growth and evolution. You can write about your thoughts, feelings, dreams, and experiences.

Shadow Work: Shadow work involves consciously exploring and integrating our Shadow. This process, although challenging, leads to greater self-awareness, self-acceptance, and personal growth. Techniques for shadow work can range from journaling and dream analysis to guided meditations and therapeutic practices.

Sacred Spaces: Create a sacred space in your home for meditation and reflection. This could be a small corner with a cushion for meditation, a shelf with items that have spiritual significance to you, or an entire room dedicated to your spiritual practice.

Community: Seek out like-minded individuals or communities who are also on a spiritual path. This can provide a sense of belonging and support and can offer opportunities for learning and growth.

Entheogenic Exploration: If you feel called and it's legal in your jurisdiction, consider exploring the use of entheogens (psychoactive substances / Sacred Medicine used in a shamanic context) for spiritual growth and healing. Do this under the guidance of a knowledgeable and trustworthy guide!

Breath Work: Harness the transformative power of breath work to journey into spiritual dimensions. Through controlled and rhythmic breathing techniques, you can transcend the confines of the physical realm, tapping into deeper states of consciousness and spiritual insights.

Continuous Learning: Keep an open mind and remain a lifelong learner. Delve into books, attend workshops or courses, and listen to lectures or podcasts that can expand your understanding of the self, the universe, and the spiritual path.

Service (Karma Yoga): Look for opportunities to serve others. This could be through volunteering, helping a neighbor, or simply offering a kind word when someone needs it. Acts of service can be a powerful way to cultivate compassion and interconnectedness.

Sketching: This practice transcends mere drawing; it is a manifestation technique that allows us to visualize our intentions with clarity and focus. When we sketch, we engage in a dialogue with the universe, outlining our desires on the canvas of reality. Each line drawn with purpose channels our energy toward the creation of our intent. By visualizing our goals and inscribing them onto paper, we solidify the ephemeral thoughts into tangible blueprints. This act is more than a draft; it is a commitment to our purpose, a visual affirmation that what we conceive can indeed become real. Thus, sketching is not only a step in the design process - it is a ritual that bridges the gap between potentiality and actuality. When we sketch with intent, we set the wheels of the universe in motion, propelling ourselves toward the manifestation of our personal destiny. *"Study the science of art. Study the art of science. Develop your senses- especially learn how to see. Realize that everything connects to everything else"* - Leonardo da Vinci

Remember, the journey of spiritual growth and self-discovery is a personal one, and different practices will resonate with different individuals. Listen to your intuition, trust your journey, and embrace the adventure, but don't listen to your ego and if you are scared, it's your Ego!

Retreat ideas to learn to navigate the karmic multiverse

1. Himalayan Meditation Retreats

Location: Dharamshala, India

Focus: Deep meditation, yogic practices, and ancient Vedic teachings.

Activities: Guided meditation sessions, yoga classes, nature walks, and spiritual discourses by revered gurus.

Duration: 7 to 21 days.

2. Sacred Geometry Workshops

Location: Sedona, Arizona, USA

Focus: Understanding and harnessing the power of sacred geometry.

Activities: Hands-on workshops on creating sacred geometric patterns, meditations within geometric installations, and discussions on their cosmic significance.

Duration: 3 to 5 days.

3. Crystal Healing Retreat

Location: Minas Gerais, Brazil

Focus: Tapping into the vibrational energies of crystals.

Activities: Crystal mining, guided meditations with crystals, workshops on crystal grids, and energy healing sessions.

Duration: 10 days.

4. Forest Bathing Retreats (Shinrin-Yoku)

Location: Kyoto, Japan

Focus: Immersing oneself in the healing energies of the forest.

Activities: Guided forest walks, mindful breathing exercises, meditation by waterfalls, and traditional tea ceremonies.

Duration: 5 to 7 days.

5. Astral Projection Workshops

Location: Glastonbury, UK

Focus: Exploring the astral realms and understanding out-of-body experiences.

Activities: Guided astral projection sessions, discussions on dream realms, and energy cleansing rituals.

Duration: 4 days.

6. Sacred River Retreats

Location: Rishikesh, India

Focus: Spiritual rejuvenation by the sacred Ganges river.

Activities: Daily yoga sessions, Ganges aarti (fire ceremony), meditation by the river, and Satsangs (spiritual discourses).

Duration: 7 to 14 days.

7. Desert Solitude Retreats

Location: Sahara Desert, Morocco

Focus: Finding inner peace and clarity in the vastness of the desert.

Activities: Sand meditation, camel treks, nightly campfires with traditional music, and stargazing sessions.

Duration: 6 to 10 days.

8. Cacao Ceremonies and Retreats

Location: Oaxaca, Mexico

Focus: Heart-opening ceremonies using ceremonial-grade cacao.

Activities: Cacao rituals, guided group meditations, traditional dances, and sharing circles.

Duration: 3 to 5 days.

9. Holotropic Breathwork Retreats

Location: Canton of Fribourg in Switzerland

Focus: Accessing non-ordinary states of consciousness for healing and self-exploration through breathwork.

Activities: Guided holotropic breathwork sessions, integrative sharing circles, supportive bodywork, and conscious integration practices.

Duration: 1 to 7 days

10. Sound Healing Retreats

Location: Ubud, Bali, Indonesia

Focus: Harnessing the healing power of sound and vibration.

Activities: Gong baths, Tibetan singing bowl sessions, vocal toning workshops, and traditional Balinese music performances.

Duration: 7 days.

11. Shamanic Sacred Medicine Retreats

Location: Amazon jungle, Peru, Brazil or the mountains of Colombia

Focus: Engaging with ancient shamanic practices and plant medicines.

Activities: Ceremonial Ayahuasca journeys, Kambo medicine sessions, ancestral healing rituals, root healing and integration circles.

Duration: 8 to 14 days.

12. Dark Room Retreats

Location: Lake Atitlán, Guatemala

Focus: Deep spiritual immersion in the heart of Mayan lands, using the veil of darkness to connect with ancient energies and inner wisdom.

Activities: Guided meditations, ancestral Mayan rituals, breathwork sessions for spiritual experiences, and post-retreat integration circles.

Duration: 10 to 20 days.

13. Traditional Yoga Ashram Stays

Location: India

Focus: Immersion in traditional yogic practices and philosophies.

Activities: Daily Ashtanga or Hatha yoga sessions, pranayama (breathwork), scriptural studies, karma yoga (selfless service), and satsangs.

Duration: 14 days to 3 months.

14. Shamanic Drumming Circles

Location: Taos, New Mexico, USA

Focus: Using drum rhythms to achieve altered states of consciousness and spiritual awakening.

Activities: Group drumming sessions, spirit animal journeys, and fire ceremonies.

Duration: 3 to 5 days.

15. Sacred Dance Retreats

Location: Bali, Indonesia

Focus: Using dance as a form of spiritual expression and healing.

Activities: Ecstatic dance sessions, movement meditation, and workshops on embodying different energies through dance.

Duration: 1 - 7 days.

16. Vipassana Meditation Retreats

Location: Various locations worldwide

Focus: Intense silent meditation focusing on the deep interconnection between mind and body.

Activities: 10 days of silent meditation, daily discourses, and individual practice.

Duration: 10 days.

17. Sacred Fire Circles

Location: Upstate New York, USA

Focus: Harnessing the transformative power of fire in a communal setting.

Activities: Group chanting, drumming, dancing around the sacred fire, and sharing circles.

Duration: 3 days.

18. Awareness Through the Body (ATB) Workshops

Location: Auroville, India

Focus: Cultivating self-awareness, concentration, and relaxation through sensory exploration and mindful movement.

Activities: Engaging in exercises that enhance attention, refine the senses, and promote the integration of mind, body, and emotions. Participants also explore different planes of existence and experience various aspects of their being, such as the subtle physical, vital, and mental bodies.

Duration: Varies; workshops range from weekend sessions to intensive programs.

19. Cenote Spiritual Cleansing Retreats

Location: Yucatán Peninsula, Mexico

Focus: Engaging in spiritual cleansing rituals in the sacred cenotes (natural sinkholes).

Activities: Guided swims in cenotes, Mexican-Mayan purification ceremonies, and meditation by the water.

Duration: 5 to 7 days.

20. Tibetan Singing Bowl Healing Retreats

Location: Kathmandu Valley, Nepal

Focus: Using the harmonious sounds of Tibetan singing bowls for healing and meditation.

Activities: Sound baths, workshops on playing the bowls, and guided meditations enhanced by the bowls' resonances.

Duration: 7 days.

Glossary

Akashic Records: Theoretical compendium of all human events, thoughts, words, emotions, and intent ever to have occurred in the past, present, or future, believed to be encoded in the astral plane.

Alchemy: An ancient tradition aiming to transmute base elements into noble ones, like gold. Metaphorically, it represents the transformative journey from ignorance to enlightenment.

Alchemy of Emotions: The process of transmuting our emotions, especially those that are negative or uncomfortable, into wisdom, learning, and personal growth.

Akasha (Ether): In Hindu philosophy - especially in Ayurveda, Yoga, Vaisheshika and Samkhya philosophies - Akasha is considered the first and most fundamental of the five elements (Pancha Mahabhuta). Akasha is the space where the other elements (fire, air, water, earth) manifest, and it's also the field of life and consciousness.

Astral Travel: Also known as "soul travel," it refers to the experience of one's consciousness leaving the physical body to travel in the astral plane. This can be done through meditation, breathwork or responsible use of entheogens.

Atman: A term used in Hindu philosophy referring to the innermost essence, the individual soul or self, which is considered eternal and divine.

Back-Fill / Back-Drop People: In certain metaphysical contexts, these terms are used to describe individuals who, from this perspective, are considered to have a less complex consciousness or soul. They are individuals who blend into the background of other people's experiences, often displaying predictable or routine patterns of behavior.

Bardo: In Tibetan Buddhism, it refers to the intermediate state between death and rebirth.

Brahman: In Hindu philosophy, the ultimate reality or supreme cosmic power.

Conscious Consumption: The practice of making choices, both in terms of physical consumption like food and mental consumption like media, that are beneficial to one's well-being and aligned with one's values.

Conscious Reality Creation: The idea that we actively participate in the creation and transformation of reality through our intentions, thoughts, emotions, and actions.

Cosmic Dance: The metaphorical dance of energies, frequencies, and consciousness that creates and sustains the multiverse.

Cosmic Choreography: A metaphor for the intricate and harmonious interactions between all elements of the multiverse, including energies, frequencies, and consciousness.

Dhikr: A devotional practice in Sufism that involves the repetitive chanting of divine names.

Ether (or Aether): In ancient and medieval science, ether (also spelled aether) was the material that filled the region of the universe above the terrestrial sphere. In some modern contexts, it can refer to a space-filling substance or field.

Etheric Field: Also known as the "Akashic Field" or "A-field," it is an invisible field that connects everything in the universe, serving as a template for physical reality and a bridge between the material world and the spiritual realm.

Enlightenment: In spiritual contexts, it refers to the realization or understanding of the true nature of reality, often accompanied by a state of profound peace.

Entheogens: Psychoactive substances that induce alterations in perception, mood, consciousness, cognition, or behavior for the purposes of engendering spiritual development or healing.

General Relativity: Einstein's theory that describes gravity as the curvature of space-time caused by mass and energy.

Heterarchy: A system of organization where elements are unranked or where they possess the potential to be ranked in a number of different ways. It contrasts with a hierarchical system by promoting a flexible, decentralized structure of interdependent elements.

Higher Self: The deepest, most authentic essence of a person. It transcends the individual's ego-driven identity and connects them with the universal consciousness.

Holographic Principle: A theoretical concept suggesting that the entire universe can be seen as a two-dimensional information structure "painted" on the cosmological horizon, such that the three-dimensional world we experience is a holographic projection of this information.

Holotropic: Derived from the Greek holos (whole) and trepein (to move toward), holotropic refers to states of consciousness oriented toward wholeness and inner integration. Popularized by Stanislav Grof, it describes non-ordinary states that can catalyze deep healing, spiritual awakening, and connection with the greater Self.

Indra's Net: A metaphor used in Hindu and Buddhist philosophies to illustrate the concepts of emptiness, dependent origination, and interpenetration.

Infodynamics: A framework that combines information theory and thermodynamics to study the accumulation of information constraints during the development of dissipative structures. It explores the connection between information and entropy production, highlighting the isomorphism between physical entropy as disorder and informational entropy as variety.

Integral Yoga: Developed by Sri Aurobindo, Integral Yoga is a comprehensive yogic system that aims to harmonize all aspects of human life. It seeks to unify body, mind, and spirit, facilitating an evolutionary transformation toward divine consciousness.

Intention: A conscious mental determination or plan to carry out a specific action or achieve a particular outcome.

Karma: A principle of cause and effect where the intent and actions of an individual influence the future of that individual. Past Karma is the accumulated memory.

Karmic Imprints: Also known as "samskaras" in Hindu and Buddhist philosophies. They are the impressions left on the subconscious mind by experiences in this life or past lives, which then influence future responses and behavior.

Karma Yoga: This is a form of yoga based on the teachings of the Bhagavad Gita, where selfless action is emphasized. It encourages practitioners to act without attachment to the results of their actions, viewing every task as a path to spiritual growth and self-realization.

Luminiferous Ether: A historical concept, the hypothetical medium for the propagation of light, which was discarded with the advent of Einstein's theory of relativity.

Lila: In Hindu philosophy, the divine play of creation, where the universe is God's canvas for an endless dance of joy and creativity.

Mantra: A word, sound, or phrase repeated during meditation to aid concentration. Utilized either audibly or internally, mantras create a rhythm that promotes calmness. Each mantra carries a unique vibrational frequency. By chanting a mantra, individuals can connect with these specific frequencies, invoking associated states of consciousness.

Meditation: A practice where an individual uses a technique – such as mindfulness or focusing the mind on a particular object, thought, or activity – is used to train attention and awareness, achieving a mentally clear and emotionally calm state.

Mindful Navigation: The practice of navigating our life's journey with mindfulness, being fully present and aware in each moment.

Muraqaba: A Sufi word that means "to watch over" or "to take care of". It refers to the practice of vigilant self-observation.

Moksha: A concept in Hindu philosophy referring to liberation from the cycle of birth and death. It represents the ultimate goal of human life, the realization of one's unity with the supreme reality.

Multiverse: A concept proposing the existence of multiple or infinite universes, including our own. This includes parallel universes with different outcomes, daughter universes for every decision outcome, mathematical universes for every mathematical structure, and quantum universes for each quantum possibility.

Non-locality: A quantum principle where entangled particles influence each other instantaneously regardless of the distance separating them, challenging traditional notions of space and time.

Observer Effect: A theory in quantum physics that suggests that the act of observation can influence the phenomenon being observed.

Personal Universe: The unique universe that each conscious being creates and shapes through their karmic evolution.

Placebo Effect: The placebo effect is a psychological phenomenon where a person experiences a perceived improvement in their condition due to their belief in the effectiveness of a treatment, even if it's inactive or neutral.

Prana: In Indian spiritual traditions, Prana is the universal energy that flows in currents in and around the body as in breath.

Quantum-Karmic Multiverse Resonance: A proposed theory that every conscious being, through their karmic evolution, shapes and molds their personal universe, thereby contributing to the grand symphony of the multiverse.

Quantum Entanglement: A quantum mechanical phenomenon in which the quantum states of two or more objects are linked together so that one object can no longer be adequately described without full mention of its counterpart.

Quantum Field Theory (QFT): The theoretical framework for constructing quantum mechanical models of subatomic particles in particle physics and quasiparticles in condensed matter physics. It is a set of ideas that provides a way of envisioning and calculating quantum mechanics' behavior.

Quantum Mechanics: A fundamental theory in physics that provides a description of the physical properties of nature at the scale of atoms and subatomic particles.

Quantum Vacuum: Unlike a classical empty space, the quantum vacuum is subject to fluctuations due to the uncertainty principle. It's a state with the lowest possible energy, the ground state, where no more energy can be removed.

Quantum Gravity: A field of theoretical physics that seeks to describe gravity according to the principles of quantum mechanics.

Reincarnation: The philosophical or religious belief in an aspect of the self or soul being reborn in a different form after biological death.

Regenerative: Pertaining to practices and principles that restore, renew, and revitalize their own sources of energy and materials, often applied to sustainable agriculture, economies, and communities in the global movement toward holistic and ecological resilience.

Resonance: The phenomenon in which an external force or a vibrating system reinforces or prolongs the oscillations of another system at a specific frequency, resulting in an amplified response.

Sacred Geometry: Geometry used in the planning and construction of religious structures such as churches, temples, mosques, religious monuments, altars, and tabernacles.

Sadhana: Derived from Sanskrit, sadhana refers to a spiritual practice or discipline aimed at achieving spiritual growth or realization. This can encompass a range of activities such as meditation, yoga, chanting, prayer, or other forms of devotion, with the purpose of refining the self and attaining a state of higher consciousness.

Samskaras: In Hindu and yogic philosophy, these are mental impressions, recollections, or psychological imprints.

Samsara: The cycle of birth, death, and rebirth in Hindu, Buddhist, Jain, and Sikh philosophies. It's the worldly cycle of existence that souls are believed to traverse until achieving enlightenment or Moksha.

Satsang: A word which comes from Sanskrit, meaning "to associate with true people," to be in the company of true people - sitting with a guru, or in a group meeting seeking that association.

Shamanism: A range of traditional beliefs and practices concerned with communication with the spiritual world. A practitioner of shamanism is known as a shaman, who is believed to interact with spirit forces and channel these energies into the physical world for healing or other purposes.

Simulation Theory: A modern philosophical and scientific concept proposing that reality as we know it might be a simulated or virtual reality, akin to a computer simulation.

Sohbet: A form of dialogue in Sufism, a mystical conversation, usually one-on-one.

Soul Travel: Another term for astral projection, soul travel refers to the experience of one's consciousness or soul leaving the physical body to travel in the astral realm.

Shadow (Psychological): A term coined by Carl Jung, referring to the unconscious parts of our personality that we disown or reject.

Sufism: The mystical Islamic belief system or dimension characterized by particular values, ritual practices, doctrines, and institutions, which began very early in Islamic history and represents the main manifestation and the most important and central crystallization of mystical practice in Islam.

Suggestion (Power of Suggestion): The power of suggestion refers to the psychological phenomenon in which people are influenced by subtle cues, statements, or other forms of communication that shape their thoughts, feelings, and behaviors.

Supermind: In Integral Yoga, the term refers to a higher level of consciousness that transcends the limitations of the human mind. It represents a state of perfect knowledge, will, and bliss, where the individual consciousness is united with the Divine consciousness.

Synchronicities: Coined by Carl Jung, these are "meaningful coincidences" - events that are not causally related yet carry a significant connection for the individual experiencing them.

Tantra: A diverse tradition originating from ancient India, that uses a range of practices, including meditation, mantra, yantra, and ritual, to unite the material and spiritual worlds for spiritual understanding and growth.

Taoism: An ancient Chinese philosophy and spiritual practice that emphasizes living in harmony with the Tao, understood as the fundamental nature of the universe.

Tariqah: The spiritual path in Sufism that leads to the ultimate truth.

Tat Tvam Asi: A Sanskrit phrase, translated as "Thou art That," suggesting that the self, in its original, pure, primordial state, is wholly or partially identifiable or identical with the Ultimate Reality.

Theory of Everything (ToE): A hypothetical framework that fully explains and links together all physical aspects of the universe, uniting the forces of nature at the smallest quantum level to the largest cosmological scale.

Unified Field: A fundamental concept in quantum physics, the Unified Field represents the origin of all particles and forces in the universe. It symbolizes the profound interconnectedness of all matter and energy, emphasizing the inseparability of all phenomena within the cosmos.

Unified Field Theory: A type of ToE that seeks to describe the fundamental forces, or interactions, between subatomic particles as manifestations of a single, underlying field.

Unconditional Love: Unconditional love refers to a pure form of affection without any limitations or conditions. It's often associated with an unwavering love that is steadfast and enduring, regardless of circumstances or behaviors, embodying the highest form of love, compassion, and empathy.

Vedanta: Vedanta is a profound spiritual philosophy rooted in the ancient scriptures of India, emphasizing the oneness of existence, the divinity of the soul, and the harmony of all religions. It encompasses various paths, such as Bhakti Yoga (path of love and devotion), Jnana Yoga (path of knowledge), Karma Yoga (path of selfless work), and Raja Yoga (path of mental discipline and inner mastery)

Vertical Time: A multidimensional perspective of time in which all moments - past, present, future, and parallel - exist simultaneously within the eternal now. In Vertical Time, present Karma can reshape not only the future but also retroactively alter the past and attract entire timelines aligned with that new truth.

Vipassana: An ancient Indian meditation technique meaning "insight" or "clear seeing." It uses focused attention on the breath or bodily sensations to foster a deep understanding of reality, promoting mindfulness and equanimity.

Yantra: A mystical diagram, mainly from the Tantric traditions of the Indian religions. They are used for worship, devotion, and meditation, and the word literally means "machine" or "instrument".

Yoga: A group of physical, mental, and spiritual practices or disciplines that originated in ancient India. Practices of yoga are meant to unite, to connect, the Human with her/himself, with Nature, with Others, and with the Divine.

Yogi: A practitioner of yoga, often implying a level of mastery over the physical postures and a deep understanding of the spiritual principles of yogic philosophy.

Zen: A school of Buddhism that emphasizes meditation and the mindful acknowledgment of emotions and thoughts without judgment

About the Author

Nadim Hamdan's journey gives testimony to the transformative power of exploration, both within and beyond the self. For a decade, he was a cog in the wheel of the German corporate machinery, navigating its relentless pursuit of profits. However, beneath the professional facade, a revolutionary spirit was brewing, craving a deeper connection with existence and a more regenerative way of living.

The discovery of self-organization and decentralized governance marked a significant turning point in Nadim's life. This was more than a professional revelation - it was a key that opened the door to radical transformation. It marked his departure from capitalist norms and ushered him into a realm where nature restoration and holistic regeneration were not mere afterthoughts, but core principles. His professional interest in the future of Information Technology and computing, especially the revolutionary realm of quantum computing, drew him into the intricacies of quantum mechanics, the foundational science that underpins this book.

Guided by the wisdom of the great entheogenic masters, Nadim chose to break free from societal conventions. He let go of material possessions and embarked on a global spiritual journey. His journey took him to the Orient, where he delved into the mystical wisdom of Sufism. He explored teachings of unconditional love, tolerance, and spiritual enlightenment, challenging mainstream narratives about existence.

Nadim's travel then led him to South America and the Amazon jungle's heart. For over two years, he lived among shamans and indigenous tribes, not merely learning but actively participating in their traditions.

He contributed to the evolution of intentional communities and regenerative local currencies across South America, bringing principles of self-governance and regenerative living to life.

In a surprising turn of events, the shamans guided him to continue his journey in India. He followed their advice, immersing himself in traditional yoga retreats in the Himalayas, the ancient city of Varanasi, and spiritual ashrams in South India. These experiences provided him with profound insights into existence, consciousness, and the harmonious dance of life and nature.

This unique blend of formal education and experiential knowledge led Nadim to dedicate his life to deeply exploring conscious co-creation and regenerative living. Along his journey, he discovered the potential of AI Large Language Models. These advanced AI tools have been beneficial in assisting him in collating, organizing, and structuring the wide knowledge and rich experiences he has gleaned over the years, especially considering English is not his first language.

Nadim's intense spiritual journey is a live expression of the transformative power of exploration, courage, and openness. His experiences paint a vivid picture of the potential that lies within each of us - to question, to seek, to grow, and to dance our unique dance within the grand choreography of the Karmic Multiverse.

Afterword

As we close the pages of The Quantum-Karmic Multiverse book, we do not reach an end - we return, gently, to the great dance floor of existence. The music of the cosmos has not ceased; it plays on, subtle and ever-present, inviting us to continue dancing, continue exploring, and continue growing. What we have shared in these pages is not a conclusion, but a threshold - a beginning. A springboard into deeper layers of the mystery.

It was a great honor for me to be able to share this book with you and the distilled wisdom gathered from many sacred sources: the ancient voices of the shamanic Teacher Trees, the deep healing of entheogenic ceremonies, the quiet teachings of yoga ashrams, and the living systems thinking from regenerative and decentralized practice. All of these streams point to one ocean: a world where harmony with nature, equity among beings, and a spiritual coherence across all layers of reality is not only possible, but emergent.

As you continue your own sacred journey, may you carry with you the subtle codes of conscious co-creation, the alchemical power of emotion, the catalytic force of relationships, and the refinement born of challenge. May you remember the interconnectedness of all that is, the infinite dance of the quantum-karmic multiverse, and the timeless whispers carried within the Aether. But most of all, remember: this journey is yours. It unfolds through your choices, your rhythm, your medicine, your joy.

This path is not for everyone. It is not always easy, linear, or comfortable. But if you choose to walk it - if you say yes to the deep inner work it asks - you may discover that you are what some call an Anchor Being. One who grounds the sacred in their personal universe. One who gives life force and coherence to the reality they inhabit. If you feel that stirring, I invite you to reach out. We are gathering an Anchor Circle - a constellation of souls committed to navigating the multiverse in resonance. We meet in Heart Sharing Circles and Spiritual Consensus Circles, where truth is not imposed, but revealed together.

After all my searching, synthesis, and in the final analysis, we can now say: in the Multiverse, Purpose is the Boss, and Consensus is the Truth.

The dance continues. The music plays on. And I look forward to seeing where your steps take you next. In this cosmic choreography, every beat holds a story, and every dancer is a star. So keep dancing - with presence, humility, and joy.

With love and gratitude ♡

Nadim Hamdan

PS. If you want to have more practical insights,
I invite you to read this book:

"How to Build a Regenerative Village"

https://treehousedao.earth/

Further Reading

1. Wheeler, J. A. (1998). Geons, Black Holes & Quantum Foam: A Life in Physics. W. W. Norton & Company.

2. Amit Goswami PhD. Quantum Spirituality: The Pursuit of Wholeness

3. Michael A Singer - 'the untethered soul'

4. Hawking, S. (1988). A Brief History of Time. Bantam Dell Publishing Group.

5. Kaku, M. (1994). Hyperspace: A Scientific Odyssey Through Parallel Universes, Time Warps, and the 10th Dimension. Oxford University Press.

6. Radin, D. (2006). Entangled Minds: Extrasensory Experiences in a Quantum Reality. Paraview Pocket Books.

7. Tolle, E. (2005). A New Earth: Awakening to Your Life's Purpose. Penguin Group.

8. Zukav, G. (1979). The Dancing Wu Li Masters: An Overview of the New Physics. HarperCollins.

9. Goswami, A. (1995). The Self-Aware Universe: How Consciousness Creates the Material World. Penguin Group.

10. Laszlo, E. (2004). Science and the Akashic Field: An Integral Theory of Everything. Inner Traditions.

11. Penrose, R. (2004). The Road to Reality: A Complete Guide to the Laws of the Universe. Vintage Books.

12. Prabhupada, A.C.B.S. (1972). Bhagavad-gita As It Is. The Bhaktivedanta Book Trust.

13. Sagan, C. (1980). Cosmos. Random House.

14. Talbot, M. (1991). The Holographic Universe. Harper Perennial.

15. Tarnas, R. (2006). Cosmos and Psyche: Intimations of a New World View. Plume.

16. Wilber, K. (2000). A Theory of Everything: An Integral Vision for Business, Politics, Science, and Spirituality. Shambhala Publications.

17. Zukav, G., & Francis, L. (2010). The Seat of the Soul. Free Press.

18. Chopra, D. (2006). Life After Death: The Burden of Proof. Harmony.

19. Davies, P. (1984). Superforce: The Search for a Grand Unified Theory of Nature. Simon & Schuster.

20. Hawking, S., & Mlodinow, L. (2010). The Grand Design. Bantam Books.

21. Lovelock, J. (1979). Gaia: A New Look at Life on Earth. Oxford University Press.

22. Murphy, M., & White, R. A. (1995). In the Zone: Transcendent Experience in Sports. Penguin Arkana.

23. Planck, M. (1931). Where is Science Going?. Norton & Company.

24. Sheldrake, R. (1981). A New Science of Life: The Hypothesis of Formative Causation. Blond & Briggs.

25. Smolin, L. (2001). Three Roads to Quantum Gravity. Basic Books.

26. Tiller, W. A. (1997). Science and Human Transformation: Subtle Energies, Intentionality and Consciousness. Pavior.

27. Wheeler, J. A., & Ford, K. (1998). Geons, Black Holes, and Quantum Foam: A Life in Physics. W. W. Norton & Company.

28. Bohr, N. (1934). Atomic Theory and the Description of Nature. Cambridge University Press.

29. Goswami, A. (2001). Physics of the Soul: The Quantum Book of Living, Dying, Reincarnation and Immortality. Hampton Roads Publishing.

30. Greene, B. (2004). The Fabric of the Cosmos: Space, Time, and the Texture of Reality. Knopf.

31. Herbert, N. (1985). Quantum Reality: Beyond the New Physics. Anchor Books.

32. Kaku, M. (2008). Physics of the Impossible: A Scientific Exploration into the World of Phasers, Force Fields, Teleportation, and Time Travel. Doubleday.

33. Laszlo, E. (1996). The Whispering Pond: A Personal Guide to the Emerging Vision of Science. Element Books.

34. Penrose, R. (1989). The Emperor's New Mind: Concerning Computers, Minds and The Laws of Physics. Oxford University Press.

35. Radin, D. (2009). The Conscious Universe: The Scientific Truth of Psychic Phenomena. HarperOne.

36. Sheldrake, R. (2012). Science Set Free: 10 Paths to New Discovery. Deepak Chopra Books.

37. Tolle, E. (1997). The Power of Now: A Guide to Spiritual Enlightenment. Namaste Publishing.

38. Wilczek, F. (2008). The Lightness of Being: Mass, Ether, and the Unification of Forces. Basic Books.

39. Zukav, G. (1989). The Seat of the Soul. Free Press.

40. Capra, F., & Luisi, P. L. (2014). The Systems View of Life: A Unifying Vision. Cambridge University Press.

41. Chopra, D., & Kafatos, M. C. (2017). You Are the Universe: Discovering Your Cosmic Self and Why It Matters. Harmony.

42. Davies, P. (1995). About Time: Einstein's Unfinished Revolution. Simon & Schuster.

43. Hawking, S. (2001). The Universe in a Nutshell. Bantam Books.

44. Lovelock, J. (2000). Homage to Gaia: The Life of an Independent Scientist. Oxford University Press.

45. Murphy, M. (1992). The Future of the Body: Explorations into the Further Evolution of Human Nature. Jeremy P. Tarcher.

46. Planck, M. (1949). Scientific Autobiography and Other Papers. Philosophical Library.

47. Sheldrake, R. (1995). Seven Experiments That Could Change the World: A Do-It-Yourself Guide to Revolutionary Science. Riverhead Books.

48. Smolin, L. (2013). Time Reborn: From the Crisis in Physics to the Future of the Universe. Houghton Mifflin Harcourt.

49. Tiller, W. A. (2007). Psychoenergetic Science: A Second Copernican-Scale Revolution. Pavior.

50. Bohm, D. (1980). Wholeness and the Implicate Order. Routledge & Kegan Paul.

51. Greene, B. (1999). The Elegant Universe: Superstrings, Hidden Dimensions, and the Quest for the Ultimate Theory. W. W. Norton & Company.

Manifesto

A Manifesto for Evolution: Guiding the Cosmic Rhythm with Unconditional Love'

Preamble:

In the grand tapestry of existence, we stand at the confluence of ancient wisdom and modern science, embarking on a journey that intertwines the mystical with the empirical. This manifesto serves as a beacon for those seeking to navigate their personal destiny in the multiverse, a guide to harmonizing the quantum-karmic dance of life.

1. Acknowledgment of Interconnectedness:

We recognize the profound interconnectedness of all existence. Just as particles in quantum mechanics exhibit entanglement, so too are our lives intricately woven into the cosmic web. Every thought, action, and intention resonates within this universal tapestry, echoing through the multiverse.

2. Embrace of Dualities:

We accept the coexistence of seemingly opposing forces – science and spirituality, chaos and order, the physical and the metaphysical. In their balance lies the harmony of existence, a dance of complementary energies that guide our journey through the multiverse.

3. Pursuit of Conscious Evolution:

We commit to conscious growth and self-transformation. Understanding that our personal universe is a reflection of our inner state, we strive for emotional mastery, mental clarity, and spiritual enlightenment. Our evolution contributes to the collective upliftment of consciousness.

4. Integration of Quantum-Karmic Principles:

We integrate the principles of quantum mechanics and karma into our daily lives, recognizing that our reality is shaped by both the observable universe and the unseen forces of action and consequence. We embrace the power of intention and the impact of our choices on our karmic path.

5. Cultivation of Mindful Awareness:

We cultivate a mindful approach to life, where attention and intention are consciously directed. We understand that where attention goes, energy flows, and thus, we choose to focus on positivity, growth, and unity.

6. Valuing of Decentralized Harmony:

We value the principle of decentralized governance as observed in nature and quantum synchronization. In our personal universes, we seek balance, allowing for the natural ebb and flow of life while contributing to collective harmony.

7. Respect for Diversity and Individual Paths:

We respect the diversity of paths and perspectives. Each journey through the multiverse is unique, and we honor the individual experiences and beliefs that contribute to the rich mosaic of existence.

8. Emphasis on Co-creation and Collaboration:

We emphasize the power of co-creation and collaborative efforts. Recognizing that our actions influence others and vice versa, we strive for constructive interactions that foster mutual growth and understanding.

9. Commitment to Regenerative Practices:

We commit to regenerative practices that promote healing, renewal, and sustainability. From personal health to environmental stewardship, our choices are guided by a desire to contribute positively to the world around us.

10. Celebration of the Cosmic Dance:

Finally, we celebrate the cosmic dance of existence, embracing the joy, mystery, and beauty of life. We recognize our role as both participants and observers in this grand ballet, and we dance with gratitude, love, and an open heart toward the infinite possibilities of the multiverse.

In this manifesto, we pledge to navigate The Quantum-Karmic Multiverse with Love, Gratitude, Wisdom, Compassion, and an unwavering quest for deeper Understanding, as we journey toward our personal and collective destiny.

Gratitude To Us